NATO AND OUT-OF-AREA ISSUES:
INTRA-ALLIANCE DYNAMICS AND THE DISCURSIVE CHANGE OF A NORM

by
Mustafa K. SAYGI

Abstract

This dissertation demonstrates that out-of-area norm's new proactive version is not completely internalized in NATO, despite 20 years of change process. Through the discursive analysis of norms change in three steps, I found that there might still be actors in the Atlantic Alliance who may prefer the old defensive and reactive version of the out-of-area norm, dating from the Cold War. The first step of emergence was successful with the U.S. executive playing the norm entrepreneur role. In the second step, the cascade of the new norm was assured via the U.K. executive's efforts as the main norm follower. However, on the last step of internalization, I show that some actors still resort to the old version of the norm to argue and justify their positions. It is an evidence which indicates how it may be difficult to change a norm that has a legal basis defended by a treaty.

Keywords: NATO, out-of-area, predicate analysis, norm entrepreneurs, discursive change, intra-alliance dynamics

"His ego nec metas rerum nec tempora pono/imperium sine fine dedi." (Vergilius, 2002 [-29 and -19] v. 278-279)

Acknowledgements

I would like to, first of all, extend my sincere gratitude to my supervisor Prof. Stephanie C. Hofmann for her support and valuable criticisms. I would also like to express my thanks to Prof. Jussi M. Hanhimäki, my second reader, for increasing my interest on transatlantic relations. My thanks go as well to all my friends in the department with whom I had an occasion to discuss my dissertation. Finally, I wish to express my deep gratitude to my family for their moral support throughout the process. All remaining errors in this study are my own.

Table of Contents

ACDA	Arms Control and Disarmament Agency
CIA	Central Intelligence Agency
CJTF	Combined Joint Task Forces
CSCE	Conference on Security and Co-operation in Europe
DOD	United States Department of Defence
DOS	United States Department of State
DPC	Defence Planning Committee
ESDI	European Security and Defense Identity
EU	European Union
HQ	Headquarters
ICTY	International Criminal Tribunal for the former Yugoslavia
ISAF	International Security Assistance Force
JCS	Joint Chiefs of Staff
NAC	North Atlantic Council
NATO	North Atlantic Treaty Organization
NIC	National Intelligence Council
NLP	Natural Language Processing
NSC	National Security Council
NSSD	National Security Studies Directives
NTC	National Transitional Council
NTM-I	NATO Training Mission-Iraq
OAPEC	Organization of Arab Petroleum Exporting Countries
OSCE	Organization for Security and Co-operation in Europe
OSD	Office of the Secretary of Defence

OVP	Office of the Vice-President
PfP	Partnership for Peace
R2P	Responsibility to Protect
SACEUR	Supreme Allied Commander Europe
SG	Secretary General
Soviet Union	Union of Soviet Socialist Republics
SOP	Standard operating procedure
U.K.	United Kingdom of Great Britain and Northern Ireland
UN	United Nations
UNPROFOR	United Nations Protection Force
UNSC	United Nations Security Council
U.S.	United States of America
USAF	United States Air Force
Warsaw Pact	Treaty of Friendship, Cooperation and Mutual Assistance
WMDs	Weapons of Mass Destruction
WWII	World War II

List of Tables and Figures

Introduction

This dissertation analyses the evolution of the out-of-area norm (Kitchen, 2010a, p. 105) in the North Atlantic Treaty Organization ('**NATO**') during the post-Cold War era, at the discursive level. I particularly demonstrate the role of the intra-alliance dynamics in this process of change and so the importance of strategic agreements amongst member countries at the political level. My argument relies on the norm entrepreneurs and norm change concepts (Finnemore & Sikkink, 1998) in international relations. Based on this, I investigate the three posited steps of a norm cycle – emergence, cascade and internalization – in the concrete case of NATO. I focus on the period from 1980 to 2011, while inspecting three specific empirical cases: the Bosnian war (1992 to 1995), the Iraq war (2003 to 2011) and the Libyan war (March 19, 2011 to October 31, 2011). For each case, I examine the discourses – via predicate analysis[1] – of the executive leaders of three types[2] of NATO member and compare it to the Secretary Generals' ones, in order to assess the different conceptions in the Alliance.[3]

The Cold War period was characterized by several international crises which presented serious challenges to the intra-alliance dynamics of NATO (Lundestad, 2003; Stuart & Tow, 1990). These out-of-area issues[4] created several camps of countries who refused to give assistance to each other on respective occasions, as important as not letting the use of NATO's airspace to an ally's planes – the United States of America ('**U.S.**') – while the Union of Soviet Socialist Republics' ('**Soviet Union**') ones could freely pass through. Hence, problems mainly opposed the U.S. to European countries, while the latter camp's homogeneity depended on the crisis in question. To be brief, Americans refused to help Europeans during the decolonization

---

[1] This specific version of a discourse analysis is presented in detail **on page 27**.

[2] The *Leading member*, a *contributing member* and an *opposing member* country to the concerned military operation in each case.

[3] The terms "NATO", "Atlantic Alliance", "Western Alliance", and "Alliance" are used indistinctly in this dissertation.

[4] The decolonization process, the Suez Crisis, the Six-Day War, the Yom Kippur War and the Vietnam War to cite the most prominent ones.

whereas Europeans made the same refusal for the Vietnam war. At the end, NATO was not directly used for any out-of-area operations[5] and the solidarity aspect seemed to be in trouble, even if the Alliance still persisted up to today. These international crises, in a certain way, were the empirical manifestations of three interconnected problems which have existed since the foundation of the Alliance: decision-making structure, burden-sharing and out-of-area issues (Croft, Howorth, Terriff, & Webber, 2000; Hanhimäki et al., 2012; Williams, 2013). The rigid consensual decision-making structure of NATO prevented the Alliance from taking any potential stances against an international crisis in due time. The burden-sharing problem between the U.S. and the European allies caused some troubles to the former one, especially during the Vietnam war[6] (Hanhimäki et al., 2012, pp. 82-83). Finally, disagreements about out-of-area issues – international crisis occurring outside of the territory covered by the Article 6 of NATO – complicated reaching a common strategic understanding towards an external affair and act in consequence: the large number of member States rarely all agreed on a subject (Stuart & Tow, 1990, pp. 13-18). As of today, there is no clear evidence that these difficulties are completely resolved.

Nevertheless, shortly after the end of the Cold War, NATO started to use its military power outside of the treaty area (Moore, 2007; Yost, 1998a). Each of these operations was decided and carried out when the classical consensual decision-making procedure was still in place and the three problems[7] cited above were not totally resolved yet (e.g., For the instauration of a No-fly zone and the supervision of an air campaign in Libya, NATO encountered several problems during the process – Turkish requests, German disagreement, reluctance from several other

---

[5] France and the United Kingdom of Great Britain and Northern Ireland ('**U.K.**') insisted for NATO's direct and active support during the Suez Crisis. By the same token, President Johnson tried to persuade European allies of the necessity to use NATO's capabilities in the Vietnam War – for this case, please see (Hanhimäki, Schoenborn, & Zanchetta, 2012, p. 82). Both of these initiatives were not successful.

[6] It is true that these troubles were more or less resolved thanks to the prevalence of disputes settlement through democratic norms inside the alliance. For further information on this characteristic, please see (Risse-Kappen, 1996).

[7] Which were always of concern for one or several member countries at different critical moments of the Alliance's history.

countries – before finally finding a way to involve itself and achieve its objectives). One may argue that these interventions are made possible by the enhanced interoperability between allies – due to common NATO exercises which have been realized since the 1950s –, facilitating the formation of coalitions and agreements. Though this argument might be true at the technical, tactical and procedural level once a real operation is put in place, it does not hold for the initial agreement on an intervention. Because to overcome high-level strategic challenges, there is a need for political decisions which can only be obtained if a consensual settlement on an issue is existent (Derleth, 2015, p. 184). Without a common resolution at the higher level, the interoperability is not useful.[8] Other major explanations also relying on material factors such as institutional adaptation (Wallander, 2000), individual incentives (Lepgold, 1998) or organizational/institutional change (McCalla, 1996) are not sufficient to shed a light on the initial political consensus step between the allied countries. Thereby, to fill this gap in the literature and given the impact of norms in alliance management (Hofmann & Yeo, 2015; Risse-Kappen, 1996), I ask the following research question:

How has the discourse on the out-of-area norm in NATO changed after the Cold War?

To answer this question, I put in place a method which will be used for the first time in this subject. Even if discourse analysis was already used in several research about norms in NATO (Behnke, 2013; Kitchen, 2010b), it did not reach a satisfying level of systematization.[9] In this study, I use predicate analysis in a sequential way to identify equivalent classes for different discursive subjects (e.g., NATO, the country itself, the coalition, etc.). This permits to assess the change process of the out-of-area norm in a comparative and transparent way.

---

[8] This apologia is, of course, valid only for the general and formal involvement of NATO in an out-of-area issue. Interoperability without a common high-level strategic decision might still be useful for allied members to form ad hoc coalitions of the willing.

[9] In fact, the authors in both of these studies use discourse analysis without specific technic, procedures and rules. This leaves too much room for subjective interpretations.

This dissertation is organized as follows. In the next section, I present the content of the out-of-area norm and its emergence during the Suez Crisis. After, I propose a literature review on NATO's change of attitude towards out-of-area issues in the post-Cold War context, especially focusing on three major rationales: institutional adaptation, individual incentives and organizational/institutional change. A critical section shows the existing gaps in the literature and details how this dissertation contributes to filling it out. Next, I specify my theoretical basis. I set out the general norm entrepreneurs/change argument whilst also explicating how the mechanism applies to my specific case of study. After that, I display the methodological structure of my work. A section introduces the general inferential scheme composed of the period of analysis, the case selection, the unit of analysis and sources. Another one lays out the qualitative method of analysis consisting of two branches: archival analysis and predicate analysis done via a Natural Language Processing ('**NLP**') toolkit. Then I move on to the results and analysis part where I present and discuss the empirical data in five sub-chapters. *First*, I relate the findings of my archival analysis[10] which shows the status of the out-of-area norm debate in NATO during the late-Cold War. *Second*, I start with the discourse analysis of my first case: the Bosnian war. *Third,* I do the same with the Iraq war. *Fourth,* I finish the analysis of my cases with the Libyan war. *Fifth,* I make some final remarks about the findings and answer the research question. Lastly, I conclude the dissertation with a summary, accompanied by paragraphs about the contribution and limitations of the study, and a prolongation for future research.

I) The emergence of the out-of-area norm in NATO

The origins of the out-of-area norm in NATO go back to the Suez crisis in 1956 (Kitchen, 2010a; Liland, 1999, pp. 63-74). The process of its emergence started with the nationalization

---

[10] From the Central Intelligence Agency's ('**CIA**'), the United States Department of State's ('**DOS**') and NATO's archives.

of the Suez Canal by Nasser and Israeli invasion as a response, followed by an Anglo-French military support. After the start of the fights, a big political pressure from the U.S., the Soviet Union, and the United Nations ('**UN**') resulted in the end of the conflict and the removal of troops. Later on, it became evident that the military invasion initiated by the three countries was not spontaneous but planned well before.

In this affair, the implication of British and French troops broke out a crisis in NATO with regard to "in" and "out-of-area" distinction (Kitchen, 2010a, p. 107). They did not bring this issue to the North Atlantic Council ('**NAC**'), but still asked for allied assistance by arguing that their national and Europe's security was under threat (Kitchen, 2010a, p. 107). In more concrete terms, they claimed that the nationalization of the Suez Canal constitutes a threat to their economic security and independence because of the risk over oil supply. According to them, this move was, moreover, an alarming sign of Nasser's accumulation of dictatorial power and an indication that he should immediately be stopped (Kitchen, 2010a, p. 107). The French parliament mentioned the necessity of NATO providing assistance to them because Nasser is also supplying Algerian separatists (Kitchen, 2010a, p. 107). Thence, both France and the U.K. invoked Article 5 for asking at least the acceptance of their move, even if Nasser was not directly linked to the Soviet threat against which the concerned Article was written in the NATO treaty. On their side, the U.S. and other members rejected Anglo-French requests (Kitchen, 2010a, p. 107; Liland, 1999, pp. 53-62). The Americans pointed out the senselessness of the economic security argument: the nationalization of the Suez Canal is a solvable technical issue and in any case oil would still circulate freely (Kitchen, 2010a, p. 107). Via John Foster Dulles's statement, the U.S. established a clear difference between in and out-of-area, meanwhile also defining the type of threat counter which NATO should react (Kitchen, 2010a, p. 108). By this statement, they made obsolete any future possibilities to evoke and interpret Article 5 in broad terms regarding an out-of-area issue for asking help from the Alliance. This move was more than justified for most of the other members of NATO because neither the delineation of the original treaty in 1949, nor the emergence of the out-of-area norm during the Suez crisis were independent from the decolonization process in the Third World. The U.S. being anti-colonialist in spirit at that time, did not want to be embraced in any colonial disputes (Kitchen, 2010a, p. 108). So, it did not include any colonial territories except the French Algeria.[11] France and the U.K. did not have the power and will to oppose the majority. So, they accepted the situation. This incipient hierarchy between core defence tasks and colonial issues constituted the basis for the appearance of the out-of-area norm. Concretely, the norm consists of two parts which are:

> First, it states that security issues beyond mutual defence were to be seen as secondary to the overwhelming strategic interest in defence against the Soviet Union. *The second part of the out-of-area norm had emerged by the 1980s as what Frode Liland calls a 'non-policy' on security cooperation beyond mutual defence* [emphasis added]. (Kitchen, 2010a, p. 107)

The norm clarifies NATO's purpose – how to interpret Articles 4, 5 and 6 – and limitations when also preventing future disagreements which may potentially weaken the transatlantic relationship (Kitchen, 2010a, pp. 108-109). Therefore, some ad hoc and informal ways of dealing with out-of-area issues appear in NATO. Allied members make all sorts of agreements outside of the NAC structure while confronted to out-of-area problems. For instance, they decide in some cases to indirectly support members going out-of-area by replacing their troops supposed to be in Europe (Kitchen, 2010a, p. 109). These arrangements helped the out-of-area norm to sustain until the end of the Cold War (Stuart & Tow, 1990, p. 321).

Nevertheless, from the end of 1970s to the 1980s and later on, the idea to give up the Article 6 of the NATO treaty started to gain ground amongst policymakers and experts (Stuart & Tow, 1990, p. 316). This was made possible owing to the patronage of the U.S. who was no longer

---

[11] To be more accurate, French Algeria was not formally a colonial territory at the time of the NATO treaty's preparation, but a department of France.

satisfied of the out-of-area norm content, especially because of its second part: the non-policy on out-of-area issues (Liland, 1999, p. 34). As a result of this characteristic, NATO was unable to react to very important crises such as the Yom Kippur war, the Organization of Arab Petroleum Exporting Countries' ('**OAPEC**') embargo, the Iranian Revolution, the Soviet-Afghan war, and the international terrorism acts (Stuart & Tow, 1990, p. 316). It angered and troubled the U.S. who tried to initiate a change process of the norm by asking for a more active role of the Alliance in these issues. The response of the NATO bureaucracy and European members was superficial: only few statements of support were pronounced. It was well below what the U.S. was hoping for. Consequently, from the second term of Reagan's presidency until the end of the Cold War, the U.S. did not insist explicitly on the need to change the norm, even if the idea and project were still there (Stuart & Tow, 1990, p. 316). It is interesting to see the U.S. being the country who initiated the emergence process of the out-of-area norm during the Suez Crisis and, at the same time, the one who wanted it to change several decades later.

II)   Literature review

This chapter briefly reviews the literature related to my research question on the discursive change of the out-of-area norm. Given its very specific nature, the subject is most of the time indirectly addressed in works about the sustainability or decline of NATO in general. Basically, there are two groups of searchers working on the Atlantic Alliance's relevance in the post-Cold War context: the first one argues that the Alliance is still a viable security organization in the post-Cold War context (Mihalache, 2017) while the second one assumes that it is declining and is no longer a military alliance (Parenti & Adda, 2017; Rynning, 2005, p. 3). In my case, I naturally focus my attention on the first group and choose three key texts[12] – accompanied by some other related papers – that treat my subject in a more explicit way. These papers concern

---

[12] Which are the most prominent alternative explanations in the literature about my research question.

the institutional adaptation of the alliance, individual incentives for members and organizational/institutional change. I propose criticisms for each of them. At the end, I present the gap/dilemma in the literature and the pertinence of handling it.

One of the most convincing explanations about the persistence of the NATO alliance is, without doubt, Wallander's (2000) work on institutional assets and adaptability. According to her, during the Cold War, the Alliance developed general and specific assets besides its civilian bureaucracy. These qualities differentiated it from other alliances such as the Organization for Security and Cooperation in Europe ('**OSCE**') and the Treaty of Friendship, Cooperation and Mutual Assistance ('**Warsaw Pact**') while placing it to a very important position. Although these assets were settled during the Cold War primarily in order to cope with the Soviet Union threat, they "have undergone a great deal of adaptation" (Wallander, 2000, p. 731) to emerging new risks. The Alliance either succeeded in adapting some of its assets (e.g., the apparition of the Combined Joint Task Forces ('**CJTF**')) or did not (e.g., multi-nationality of commands and forces), when also creating new ones for the changing environment (e.g., Partnership for Peace ('**PfP**')) (Wallander, 2000, p. 731). Thus, regarding out-of-area issues, they permitted the Alliance to assume an active role in crises and conduct military operations for instance in Bosnia, Kosovo, Afghanistan, and Libya. So, allied members naturally decided to continue investing in the transformation of NATO's assets because the Alliance was the only organization capable of dealing with these issues. By the way, the apparition of these new assets is also a sign of NATO changing from a military alliance to a "security management institution" (Wallander & Keohane, 1999). This is because "Having been a successful alliance, NATO is building on the practices and networks constructed in response to threat, as resources for its adaptation to the role of international security institution." (Wallander & Keohane, 1999, p. 47).

There are also other works in the literature emphasizing the importance of institutional adaptation and flexibility. For example, Terriff (2003) points out three most essential and interrelated elements in the institutional adaptation of NATO: the European Security and Defense Identity[13] ('**ESDI**'), the CJTF and the new military command structure (Terriff, 2003, p. 39). Amongst them, the CJTF[14] is the key manifestation of the Alliance's stance adaptation to out-of-area issues and may be summarized as following: "a symbol that NATO knows where it is going and why, that it really does know what it is doing, that it does have a purpose." (Terriff, 2003, p. 39). The CJTF supported the role of NATO in the post-Cold War area. On another perspective, Hofmann and Mérand (2012) state the effects of institutional elasticity in adaptation to a changing environment. The authors define elasticity as a demonstration of strength and flexibility of an organization which permits a peaceful change in a region (Hofmann & Mérand, 2012, p. 134). And since the institutional flexibility and strength of NATO are high (Hofmann & Mérand, 2012, p. 152), it contributes to the peaceful change of the regional architecture and prevents stagnation. A recent book from Sloan (2010) also emphasizes the flexibility of NATO's mandate. According to the author, the allied members adapted the Alliance's purpose in order to meet the challenges occurring due to peaceful revolutions in former Soviet republics (Sloan, 2010, p. 7). Even though allied countries agreed and preferred to keep the collective defence function at the core of NATO's commitment, they also took into the agenda new mission priorities because of the changing international context (Sloan, 2010, p. 180). Similar arguments and points of view on institutional adaptation exist in other papers that I am not going to detail here.[15]

I think it is legitimate to address two main criticisms against this idea of "institutional adaptation". First, on a theoretical basis, Ikenberry (2001) claims the insufficiency of focusing

---

[13] *En passant*, this one is still in progress.

[14] The Combined Joint Task Force is a multinational and rapidly deployable force unit created mainly to deal with non-Article 5 missions of NATO. To learn more, please take a look at Yost (1998b, 2010).

[15] For additional information, see for example Chun (2013) and Duffield (1994).

only on assets while explaining the adaptation of NATO to the new security context. Since the Alliance is created after the victory of the World War II ('**WWII**') by the allies, it contributed to the emergence of a path dependency and became a quasi-constitutional order afterwards. Therefore, cheating – a classical problem in the liberal theory of collective action – did not make sense. Then, NATO affirmed and sustained its role of assuring "integration and stability" when transforming itself to catch on with the changing dangers (Ikenberry, 2001, p. 215 and ss.). Second, on the methodological side, the relationship postulated by the institutional adaptation argument to enlighten the maintenance of the alliance is not a self-sustained explanation in terms of variables. Wallander and other authors with the same idea are not clear on the sequence and combination of events: we cannot exactly say if it is the emergence of new threats, NATO's general/new institutional assets or the combination of the two which explains the maintenance of the Alliance (Williams, 2013, p. 352).

Another important article that is relevant for my research question is Lepgold's (1998) work about NATO's collective action problem in the post-Cold War context. In this study, he tries to assess if the adaptation of the Alliance to the new context will be successful or not by asking the following question: "Can NATO perform multilateral peace operations effectively and reliably?" (Lepgold, 1998, p. 78). In the opinion of him, member countries will not be enthusiastic in conducting non-Article 5 out-of-area missions because these do not involve directly the Alliance's territory. Based on the collective action theory (Olson, 1971), he assumes that potential out-of-area operations – because they are non-excludable public or a series of private goods (Lepgold, 1998, p. 97) – will be undersupplied attributable to free-riding (Lepgold, 1998, p. 79). To prevent this situation, Lepgold suggests NATO to find out new individual incentives for countries to execute these operations. He perceives the creation of the CJTF by the Alliance as a good initiative to promote individual incentives for members to participate in out-of-area missions. The CJTF structure might potentially be useful to stop free-riding "by providing individual incentives in the form of valued command responsibilities, and by reducing the number of participants in specific operations enough so that overlapping preferences can be identified and realized more easily" (Lepgold, 1998, p. 79). In terms of practical policy recommendations, he suggests the CJTF headquarters ('**HQ**') commanders to be given more responsibility and accountability for operations. This "decentralization" will motivate them to perform well in hope for personal rewards. They could even pressure their own governments if their career is at stake (Lepgold, 1998, p. 106).

Another expert has a different vision on individual incentives and free-riding while basing its argumentation still on the collective action. First of all, Ringsmose (2010) notes that if Lepgold's idea about free-riding was accurate, then the deployment of 100,000 soldiers in the International Security Assistance Force ('**ISAF**') would not happen. However, it did, and this is because there is a link between the core defensive functions of the alliance and out-of-area interventions. The general mechanism postulated by the author is as follows:

> when members of an alliance assume that the credibility of the security guarantees provided by their more powerful allies are dependent on their participation in out-of-area operations, they will tend to contribute to the mission regardless of the lack of direct incentives presented to them. *The perceived linkage between different alliance products thus facilitates the manning of public goods producing operations outside of Europe* [emphasis added]. (Ringsmose, 2010, p. 320)

Hence, the participation of allied members to ISAF is the manifestation of the value they assign to collective defence provided by NATO (Ringsmose, 2010, p. 320). Ringsmose conceptualizes collective defence not as a public good but as a club good whereas the U.S. as a guarantor has the ability to exclude members from profiting without paying the costs. Consequently, all members have substantial – not individual – incentives to contribute to out-of-area operations as long as the collective defence remains a club good (Ringsmose, 2010, p. 335). So, the free-riding problem supposed by Lepgold is not as serious as it seems to be.

McCalla's article (1996) about organizational and institutional change in NATO is another major work on NATO's persistence and implication in out-of-area problems after the Cold War. He makes the following enquiry: "How do alliances respond to changing strategic circumstances?" (McCalla, 1996, p. 445). Briefly, he defends the idea of the Alliance's persistence and adaptation to the new environment because of a bureaucracy which wants to perpetuate itself[16] and member countries who benefit from the structure (McCalla, 1996, pp. 470-471). First, based on the organizational theory, he postulates that NATO bureaucrats will have three sequential reactions when confronted to a change: resistance while preserving the core status quo functions, affirmation of the Alliance's merits to guarantee support and resource fluctuations, and finally adaptation to new threats when there is no other options left (McCalla, 1996, p. 458). Second, based on the international institutionalist approach, he argues that NATO member States will also have three sequential reactions when confronted to a change: reliance on existing standard operating procedures ('**SOP**') to deal with new threats, adapting the alliance to new challenges by the reorganization of resource allocation, and benefiting from NATO as a framework for partnership creation (McCalla, 1996, p. 464). Therefore, the author reaches two conclusions about NATO and alliance persistence in general:

> First, where the organizational development of an alliance is high, we would expect the impact of the loss of a threat on an alliance to be mitigated and hence slowed. […] Second, an alliance that is at the centre of a regime will respond more slowly to changes in threats than one that has not developed attendant norms, procedures, and functions. *The wider the range of functions that an alliance fulfils beyond its core defence function, the less responsive it will be to changes in the threats it faces and the more likely it is to be transformed in purpose as its external environment changes* [emphasis added]. (McCalla, 1996, p. 470)

---

[16] For additional information on self-interested and perpetuating bureaucracies in alliances, please refer to Bennett (1997) and Walt (1997). For example, after the Suez crisis, the secretary general ('**SG**') acquired new roles consisting of mediation, conciliation, etc. among member countries to facilitate cooperation. Concerning this point, please refer to Hendrickson (2006, 2010).

There are some legitimate criticisms concerning this latter work which I think deserve to be mentioned. First, regarding the organizational theory and self-sustaining bureaucracy, there is no much empirical evidence to affirm that this formal bureaucracy effectively had an impact on the conduct and decisions of member countries (Williams, 2013, p. 351). All the key decisions about the perpetuation and transformation of NATO were already in accordance with "pre-existing national interests and priorities" (Williams, 2013, p. 351). To be honest, McCalla recognizes this point and criticizes it in his paper. He admits the limits of organizational interests' autonomy compared to member countries' preferences. For instance, he illustrates this point with the following facts: downsizing and military reorganization, partnerships with other state or non-state actors and their participation in NATO missions, the decline trend in nuclear weapons plans, etc. (McCalla, 1996, p. 460). Second, it is evident that international institutionalist theory is also not a perfect explanation since it does not take into account power and domestic politics of members. McCalla demonstrates this deficiency in two events happened in the Alliance. First, NATO's wish to create the CJTF was characterized by hot debates between member countries over the command structure of this new arrangement (McCalla, 1996, p. 467). The U.S. was reluctant to place its troops under a foreign commander while France was insisting in increasing the NAC's role compared to the Supreme Allied Commander Europe's ('**SACEUR**') one during missions carried out by the CJTF.[17] Second, domestic politics always posed limits to the reorganization and downsizing of NATO's military infrastructure (McCalla, 1996, p. 467). Given allied members' national pride and hierarchical domestic military relations, most of the time bases only change locations. That being the case,

---

[17] This is because at that time, France was no longer part of NATO's military structure and *de facto* not represented in the Defense Planning Committee ('**DPC**'). This situation endured from 1966 to 1995, when France decided to rejoin the integrated military structure. During the CJTF debates, France does have a seat on the NAC (NATO's highest decision-making body) and therefore wants to have a word on that decision. For further information about France's relationship with NATO, please have a look at Hofmann (2017).

member countries' attitudes and decisions may prevent swift responses from the Atlantic Alliance to the changing environment of threats.

All of these texts summarized above lack a crucial aspect about the change of NATO's position vis-à-vis out-of-area issues: preference formation and evolution. The Alliance did not abandon its consensual decision-making process, and disagreements about out-of-area issues did not disappear because of the post-Cold War context. But despite these constant factors, the Alliance still successfully intervened in several out-of-area problems since the 1990s. I also think that NATO efficaciously adapted its structures to the new security context. However, the current literature does not propose a convincing and sufficient clarification on the initial high-level political agreements step which allowed the adaptation of dealing with out-of-area problems to begin. After all, as we have seen, member countries' interests are always the ones that prevail on other factors. A change relating to out-of-area issues must also be explained at the ideational, normative level[18] – where the interests of members can be measured[19] – and not only with material aspects. Therefore, I found it interesting to look at the out-of-area norm change in the discourse of relevant actors to add a modest complement to the existing literature about the adaptation of NATO to new threats. While analysing the process of this normative change at the discursive level, I will be able to observe the different steps of this transformation and see how the norm evolved through time. I will especially be able to answer these following sub-questions: who initiated the norm change and how? Which actors followed, which ones resisted first? How the other actors reacted to the change in the norm after the initial step? Is the norm completely internalized for all members nowadays or are there still challengers inside? If yes, are their arguments against the change same as the ones proclaimed at the first step?

---

[18] This is already done by Hofmann (2013) with a general perspective in mind but is not out-of-area and case specific.
[19] Through discourse analysis.

III)   Theoretical basis

I use constructivism as meta-theoretical basis for this dissertation. More precisely, I rely on the discursive and linguistic side of the school of thought and use it to assess norm and identity formation/change. The importance of norms is further emphasized by the logic of appropriateness. After being explained and adopted the norm entrepreneurs and normative change theory to my case, I present my general expectation on how the discursive change of out-of-area norm may be analysed as a process divided in three steps: emergence, cascade and internalization. The two main concepts in this study are *out-of-area norm* and *members' vision of NATO's purpose*.

In constructivism, norms form an important element of social action. Actors see them as a shortage/heuristic when making decisions and are influenced: norms have an impact non-negligible on the reasoning process (Kratochwil, 1989). This leads us to the logic of appropriateness which claims that the decision-making procedure is influenced by norms defining what is right or not in a situation rather than a rationalist cost/profit calculation (March & Olsen, 2013). The rules are accepted because "they are seen as natural, rightful, expected, and legitimate" (March & Olsen, 2013, p. 479). And actors follow them by conforming their attitude – either a role, an identity, a membership of a community, etc. – depending on the specificity of the situation (March & Olsen, 2013, p. 479). These rules are not frozen and may change or be replaced over time. The connection between the identity of an actor and rules corresponding to it may be based on: expert/scientific knowledge, expectations, intuitions, essence, etc. (March & Olsen, 2013, p. 479). Rules also guide actors in terms of precedents: they always include in themselves the indication of the authoritative figures able to interpret procedures (March & Olsen, 2013, p. 482). Since they are not frozen, rules change through interaction[20] with other actors and spread through economic, political and social networks.

---

[20] During which authoritative figures can play a role.

Discourse contributes to that change too (March & Olsen, 2013, p. 486). Regarding the speed of this changing process, March and Olsen make an interesting remark:

> Different rules, roles, and identities are evoked in different situations and when circumstances fluctuate fast, there may be rapid shifts within existing repertoires of behavioural rules based on institutionalized switching rules. *However, the basic repertoire of rules and standard operating procedures change more slowly. Change in constitutive rules usually requires time-consuming processes and a strong majority, a fact that is likely to slow down change* [emphasis added]. (March & Olsen, 2013, p. 487)

As we can see in this citation, they say that SOPs and basic rules are specific and cannot change rapidly. Applied to my case, I consider the out-of-area norm as being an SOP – given that it is directly based on a legal argument, extracting its legitimacy on the Article 6 of the NATO treaty – and therefore suppose that it will adopt slowly to the changing environment. This justifies my choice of studying the change process in three steps: emergence, cascade and internalization. Later in the text, authors describe the attitude of actors during the process of change and they say:

> In situations of disorientation, crisis, and search for meaning, actors are in particular likely to rethink who and what they and others are, and may become; what communities they belong to, and want to belong to; and how power should be redistributed. (March & Olsen, 2013, p. 489)

So, if as described above actors do question their – and others' – multiple identities during periods of change and crisis, then it is legitimate to look at the discourse produced by these actors in order to comprehend a normative change. Moreover, since all the actors will not answer these queries in the same manner even if they are part of a same community, there will be resistance to change from some of them at different moments of the procedure. For my case, these points justify my choice of looking at the executive leaders' discourse of NATO member countries about the out-of-area norm in three wars. I also do look at the SG's discourse in order to compare them. Given the possibility of resistance as March and Olsen implicitly underline in the precedent citation in italic, for each case, I do take countries which are against the change to see the extent and evolution of this opposition.

The theoretical basis of this dissertation is formed via Finnemore and Sikkink's work (1998) on norm dynamics and political change. In this article, the authors have three main arguments. First, they claim that the growing interest about ideational aspects in international relations is in fact a nostalgia about concerns which already existed in the past (Finnemore & Sikkink, 1998, p. 888). Norms were important during antiquity and until the behavioural turn in the discipline (Finnemore & Sikkink, 1998, p. 889). The motivation to leave aside norms was justified by measurement concerns: norms are harder to observe than numbers. Nevertheless, from 1990s onwards norms started to regain their legitimacy because of the changing international context and insufficiency of behavioural explanations (Finnemore & Sikkink, 1998, p. 890). According to the authors, a norm is "a standard of appropriate behaviour for actors with a given identity" (Finnemore & Sikkink, 1998, p. 891). It is different from an institution which is a collection of norms. The definition given above refers in reality to a prescriptive or evaluative norm. There are also, for instance, other types such as regulative norms – constrain the behaviour of actors – and constitutive norms – create new rules and identities (Finnemore & Sikkink, 1998, p. 891). Of course, since norms cannot be directly observed, we need to infer them from actors' behaviour (Finnemore & Sikkink, 1998, p. 892). Second, they state that the evolution of a norm is similar to a "life cycle" of three stages – emergence, cascade and internalization – and each step has a unique origin and mechanism of influence (Finnemore & Sikkink, 1998, p. 888). In the first stage of emergence, norm entrepreneurs – those actors who initiate a change – wish to adopt a norm because of altruism, empathy or ideational commitment. By using organizational platforms, they try to persuade other actors – internal or external – to adopt the norm. Before the second step of cascade, the norm must already be institutionalized to a certain level and a "tipping point" of adoption – a critical mass of actors – must have been reached (Finnemore & Sikkink, 1998, pp. 896-901). Then during the second stage, other persuaded actors start to adopt the norm in order to gain legitimacy, reputation and self-esteem. Those who already adopted the norm socialize the other ones to become followers of this new norm. This pressing comes rather from external actors than internal ones. Through this peer-pressure procedure, and after a certain number of adoptions, a link is created between the identity of actors and the new/changed norm. In other words, the behaviour of actors must conform to this new norm if they are from the same community (Finnemore & Sikkink, 1998, pp. 902-904). Finally, in the third stage, all the SOPs and other procedures incorporate the norm. Any remaining actors do also adopt the norm in order to conform to the new context. The institutionalization level of the new norm is the highest at this stage: it is taken for granted. Which factors do influence the emergence and/or change of norms? The authors give several examples for this point, one of them being the world time context. They say that moments of crises may push the actors to give up the norm supposed to resolve the problems and search for a new version or a completely different one (Finnemore & Sikkink, 1998, pp. 904-909). Third, they argue that the fact of opposing norms to rationality is not useful: it prevents from totally explaining important processes of social construction. In place of doing this, they propose the following: "Rationality cannot be separated from any politically significant episode of normative influence or normative change, just as the normative context conditions any episode of rational choice" (Finnemore & Sikkink, 1998, p. 888).

I apply this general theoretical basis to my case and expect the following mechanism. With the end of the Cold War and change of the international context, new threats appeared. Confronted to them, western countries had only NATO as a viable organization to deal with these new security challenges. Nevertheless, the Alliance's old out-of-area norm of non-intervention was no longer sufficient to resolve these problems. Therefore, as a norm entrepreneur, the U.S. initiated a change of this norm through persuasion of other members from the Bosnian war. After several years, the adoption level of this norm reached a peak with countries such as the U.K. conforming to it. SOPs regarding out-of-area issues also changed. Finally, I expect that the internalization of this norm by almost all members manifested itself during the Libyan war. All members – without power distinction – conformed to this new out-of-area norm and perceive it as a matter of habit.

The central concepts in this dissertation are, as said earlier, *out-of-area norm* and *members' vision of NATO's purpose*. Broadly defined, an *out-of-area problem* is any international crisis – military or humanitarian – happening outside of the concerned NATO territory as defined in Article 6 but has still a considerable impact on one or several member countries. The norm which governs these issues is the combination of all the SOPs, rules and procedures in place – either military, political or social – to deal with these problems. During the Cold War, different types of out-of-area disputes occurred. As Stuart and Tow (1990) do, I think we can legitimately categorize them in five types:

> 1. Situations in which NATO members have been concerned about the possibility of "guilt by association" with the out-of-area policies of another ally.
> 2. Situations in which one NATO member has seen another member's out-of-area actions as an infringement upon its *domaine réservé* in the Third World.
> 3. Situations in which a NATO member involved in an out-of-area campaign has solicited the direct or indirect support of other alliance members and has been rebuffed.
> 4. Situations in which the out-of-area preoccupations of a NATO member are criticized by other allies on the grounds that they are diverting attention, energies, or resources away from the alliance.
> 5. *Situations that highlight fundamental differences of opinion among NATO allies regarding the nature or implications of threats to the alliance or beyond the alliance treaty area* [emphasis added]. (Stuart & Tow, 1990, p. 9)

These five types are most of the time combined in international crises labelled as out-of-area problem. While I do not reject the other ones, my dissertation rather concerns the fifth point[21] –

---

[21] Which is the most crucial one.

definition of threat – because this is the most prevalent problem for NATO in the post-Cold

War context (Stuart & Tow, 1990, pp. 316-317). The *members' vision of NATO's purpose* is,

in general terms, the way in which allied countries define and perceive the Atlantic Alliance

(Kempf, 2010). Specifically, it is determined by five aspects that one may enquiry about the

Alliance at different occasions: the identity of the NATO alliance – who is "NATO" and who

form it? —, the activity domain of the Alliance – what it does in general and why it

accomplishes certain tasks and not others? —, the way NATO undertake its tasks – which are

the missions of the alliance? —, the geographical scope of the Atlantic Alliance's activity –

where the alliance intervenes and should intervene? – and the timing of a potential

response/intervention – when the alliance should take action if it needed to do so? For my

purpose, the questions of "where" and "why" are the most important ones and I am going to

look for them during the empirical analysis.

With the end of the Cold War, the U.S. foreign security policy experienced fundamental

changes (Blumenau, Hanhimäki, & Zanchetta, 2018).[22] The emergence of new risks and threats

accompanied by the collapse of the Soviet Union caused troubles to policymakers about

deciding on the roadmap to adopt. The security of the U.S. and the Western Alliance were

menaced by globalized and decentralized threats. In order to deal with them and adapt the

American foreign policy to the new century, the U.S. executive power adopted the ideational

commitment of the democratic peace theory and humanitarian intervention (Choi & James,

2014; Søndergaard, 2015). In general terms, the democratic peace theory postulates that liberal

democracies do not – or rarely – engage in conflict between each other (Doyle, 1983). Having

this in mind, a policy of exporting liberal values outside of the Western Alliance area in a pre-

emptive way to defuse threats became a common-sense in the U.S. To put this policy in

execution, they requested the help of the most important military alliance of the post-Cold War

---

[22] Even if some of the conversions – especially those regarding humanitarian help issues – already started to appear during Reagan or Bush administrations, explicit and big manifestations of them occurred after the Cold War.

context: NATO. To persuade other countries of the necessity to use the Alliance in this quest, they resorted to several arguments. First, Americans insisted that if NATO does not go out-of-area, it will go "out-of-business" because of its usefulness in the new context (Liebig, 1990). Second, they said because of the globalization, out-of-area issues' impact in the treaty area increased. Third, they claimed that the potential impact of failed States on their neighbours and NATO members is problematic. So, after the Cold War, the U.S. executive power branch pushed for a new version of the out-of-area norm in NATO.

Once the process of change is started by the U.S., several countries reacted. France, for example, was initially against this transformation together with some southern flank countries. Nevertheless, on the other hand, some members were very motivated to adopt the new version of the out-of-area norm in order to enhance their legitimacy and esteem (e.g., newly democratic countries such as Portugal and Spain). When the U.K. decided to conform to the new norm – moment being the tipping point, States that already adopted the new out-of-area norm peer-pressured the remaining ones to conform via formal networking. After the critical mass[23] of conforming States attained, being a member of the Alliance started to mean conforming to the new version of the norm. The pressure on the nonconforming countries increased. So, once the U.K.'s executive power branch was persuaded, an important ratification level of the new out-of-area norm occurred in NATO.

After the cascade step of the out-of-area norm's new version and some time, SOPs and basic rules about it also began to change. This means the adaptation of NATO's bureaucracy and training to the new norm. At this level, nonconforming states did also adopt it in order to not to be "excluded" – symbolically – from the community. The decision-making in the Atlantic Alliance is consensual and members are free to accept or refuse any changes. However, when there is only a small minority refusing to conform, it may be subject to informal pressures to

---

[23] It usually corresponds to 1/3 of members in any international system according to the authors. For additional information about threshold points, please have a look at (Finnemore & Sikkink, 1998, p. 901).

accept the change through bilateral meetings and informal networks. Consequently, the new norm was completely institutionalized and is taken for granted. After the change of the SOPs and basic rules, the new version is completely internalized in NATO.

To put it briefly, my general expectation is that the evolution and change of the out-of-area norm is similar to the theoretical argument of Finnemore and Sikkink (1998) about norm emergence. Since the out-of-area norm in NATO is an SOP and basic rule, it takes a long time to change and three steps – emergence, cascade and internalization – to completely install. The U.S. has the role of the norm entrepreneur and the U.K. the principal norm follower. The **Table 1** below summarizes my step-by-step expectations about the evolution of the norm.

Table 1 Expected steps of the out-of-area norm's evolution in NATO

Out-of-area norm	Step 1: Norm emergence/change (1992-1995)	Step 2: Norm Cascade (2003-2011)	Step 3: Internalization (2011-onwards)
Actors	The U.S. as a norm entrepreneur through NATO platform	The U.K. and other norm followers	The remaining minority (Southern flank, newcomers, etc.)
Motives	Democratic peace theory and humanitarian intervention commitment	Legitimacy concerns of new democracies and esteem of Anglo-Saxon cooperation (special relationship)	Conformity in order to avoid a symbolic exclusion from the community
Mechanism	Persuasion through argumentation about the new context	Socialization through formal networking in the Alliance	Peer pressure through informal networking in the Alliance

IV)   Methodology

I test my general expectation about the progress of the out-of-area norm in NATO through the empirical cases of the Bosnian war, the Iraq war and the Libyan war, with an inductive reasoning. More precisely, I use process-tracing as a general guideline for a sequential analysis (Mahoney, 2015) of the three steps already postulated (see *supra*): emergence of the new norm illustrated through the Bosnian war (1992-1995), the cascade of it demonstrated through the

Iraq war (2003-2011) and the internalization of this same norm revealed via the Libyan war (2011). For each case, I realize a predicate analysis in order to see and compare the predicates' evolution of some key discursive subjects through time and speakers. As a complement, I do a historical analysis of the out-of-area norm's status in NATO during the Cold War. In this part, I base my analysis and assumptions on documents found through archival research.

The period of analysis is from 1980 to 2011, meaning a time frame of thirty years. I chose this period because it corresponds to the appearance of the idea about a change in the existing norm – from 1980 to 1991 – and the concretization of it afterwards – from 1992 to 2011. Furthermore, the period also encompasses three of the most important out-of-area issues for NATO – Bosnia, Iraq and Libya[24] – that I use for the analysis. The period after 2011 is not directly taken into account since it is the recent past and access to data sources could have been difficult. Another reason is that after 2011, no major out-of-area problems impacted the alliance yet apart from the Syrian Civil War. But this latter is still ongoing and not finished, so I decided that it is not a good candidate for my research subject.[25] The unit of analysis in my dissertation are out-of-area problems, and the unit of observation are speeches from executive leaders.

The case selection is a non-random and information-oriented one. I chose these three cases – Bosnia, Iraq and Libya – on the basis of the maximum variation principle[26] which purpose is "to obtain information about the significance of various circumstances for case process and outcome" (Bent, 2006, p. 230). For each of these cases, I chose three NATO member countries and analysed the discourses of their executive leaders together with the SG's. The selection here is once again made on the principle of variation and I chose three types of countries for each crisis. The first type is the member country who is leading and/or has a very important role in the military operation. The second type is a member country who is contributing just as

---

²⁴ And several other crises during the Cold War.
²⁵ Even if it also has a non-negligible impact on the current intra-alliance dynamics.
²⁶ The expected "value" which varies here is the supposed status of the new out-of-area norm.

necessary to the operation. And the third type is a member who is against the military operation. Apropos the out-of-area crises, first, I chose the Bosnian war case – 1992 to 1995 – because it is one of the first major crisis in the post-Cold War context and also the first time that NATO gone out-of-area. So, I thought it might be accurate to take this case to observe the initial emergence phase of the new out-of-area norm. Second, I chose the Iraq war – 2003 to 2011 – as a control case during which NATO decided not to apply the new norm on the ground. The Alliance did not go out-of-area, but several members participated in a military expedition and before the beginning of it, potential contributions of NATO has been discussed. Hence, I think it is a good case to see if the Alliance's decision to intervene or not in an out-of-area problem had an impact on the discursive evolution of the norm. Third, I analyse the Libyan war case – 2011 – because it is the last major crisis in which NATO formally and militarily intervened. Consequently, I believe it is a satisfying case to see if the internalization phase of the new norm is terminated or not. These cases naturally follow a chronological order for permitting to see the evolution of the norm through time.

This dissertation relies mostly on primary sources: speeches and historical documents. For the historical complement part about the situation of the out-of-area norm during the Cold War, I used several memoranda, press statements and a special article. These come from the archives of the CIA, NATO and the DOS. I selected all the accessible documents featuring "out-of-area" word in their titles or at least one subtitle. At this point, some might deduce that the American origin of most of the documents establishes a bias towards the U.S. vision and decreases the objectivity of a potential analysis. Thus, one cannot say something about the state of the out-of-area norm in NATO by only assessing the American vision. Even though I find these criticisms legitimate, I think this problem is not as crucial as it seems to be. First, there is an access problem concerning the archives of other NATO member countries especially for documents on the out-of-area issues dating from the Cold War. Taking into account the sensibility of these records, these are most of the time not virtually accessible and the physical access is not facilitated either. So, even if I wanted to use the same type of documents from other members' archives, I would not be able to do so in due time limits. Second, during the Cold War, it is the U.S. who wanted to initiate a change of the out-of-area norm. Therefore, it is the same U.S. who was the most active about this subject and other member countries only reacted in a passive way (e.g., a nonresponse or non-discussion of the willingness to change). Thus, looking mostly to the U.S. originated documents is not a big issue for the purpose of this dissertation. Apart from that, all these documents are first-hand and authentic: there are no potential concerns about their pertinence. Memoranda collected from the CIA archives have some censored parts, but this is not an obstacle to understand the general idea. For the three out-of-area issue cases, I use speeches of the executive power branch leaders of chosen countries and the SGs's ones of that time. The selection process of the speeches was as follows. First, I listed all the speeches of a relevant speaker between the concerned time frame of the case (e.g., all speeches of Bill Clinton from 1992 to 1995). Second, for each speech, I looked for some keywords in the text in order to decide which paragraphs to keep and which ones to leave out (e.g., for Bill Clinton's speeches, if I found "NATO", "out-of-area", "Bosnia*", "Yugoslavia", "Milosevic", "the Western alliance" or "Europe" in a paragraph, I kept it). Third and finally, I created a corpus for each speaker composed of the relevant paragraphs extracted from his speeches. The corpuses are from two to nine pages, depending on the person. I chose the executive power branch for the discourse analysis because I think it is representative of the foreign security policy of a country. The same is true for the representativeness of the SG for NATO. Some might argue that other actors – or a combination of them – might also have an impact on the transformation of the out-of-area norm in the Alliance. Or some criticisms may point out the reductionist effect of focusing only on the executive power by not considering the effects that judicial and legislative branches may have on the change. I decided to focus only in one type of actor to more easily compare results across countries and time. Additionally, the effects of other actors than the executive power branch can be at best indirect and not directly observable, analysable. So, I think this choice is valid to some extent. Another point concerns some of the out-of-area issues for which the executive power leader of a country chosen for discourse analysis changes during the crisis. In such situations, I decided to keep the first leader. In doing so, I could have access to discourses made just before the crisis starts and those made in earlier months of the conflict. There are no power assumptions/considerations about the choice of the different countries. Regarding the Bosnian case, I use the U.S. as the leading country, Germany as the contributing one and Greece as the opposing one. That being so, speeches in this case are from Bill Clinton, Helmut Kohl, Andreas Papandreou and SG Manfred Wörner. For the Iraqi case, I use the U.K. as the leading country, Spain as the contributing one and Canada as the opposing one. Accordingly, speeches in this case are from Tony Blair, José María Aznar, Jean Chrétien and SG George Robertson. Finally, concerning the Libyan case, I use France as the leading country, Turkey as the contributing one and Czech Republic as the opposing one. Whence, speeches for this case are from Nicolas Sarkozy, Recep Tayyip Erdoğan, Václav Klaus and the SG Anders Fogh Rasmussen. The speeches of the SGs are extracted from the NATO speeches & transcripts archive. And the U.S. presidents' ones are collected from "The American Presidency Project" database. Other discourses are from several online repositories. Once again, these documents are original, authentic and not censored: there is no problem with regard to their pertinence.

The method for the historical complement part is archival analysis. Each memorandum, press statement and the special article are analysed accompanied by the presentation of their authors, origins, publisher, production date, publication date and the context in which they have been produced. I compare them between each other[27] and also take into consideration the bias

---

[27] Based on their stance towards the old version of the out-of-area norm.

towards the U.S. vision when commenting them. The method for the three out-of-area issues is discourse analysis. I chose discourse analysis for my dissertation because it is an important method to study the articulation of policy applications amongst decision makers, even if it leaves out the implementation process (Milliken, 1999, p. 240). Precisely, I use predicate analysis which is also known to be adapted for the study of subjects similar to mine (Milliken, 1999, p. 231). The analysis only depends on the occurrence of morphemes as distinct entities: the knowledge of the meaning of each is not necessary (Harris, 1952, p. 1). This analysis of occurrence concerns only a text in itself compared to other elements on it without taking into account any additional language elements. This procedure permits to have an insight on the interrelations between several morphemes which say something about the structure of a text in general (Harris, 1952, p. 1). It also means that some general patterns can appear for particular discursive subjects and so on. Given that different discourses mean different patterns of discursive subjects and styles, they are comparable for a purpose of analysis (Harris, 1952, p. 1). In this method of predicate analysis, the most important concept is "equivalence classes". The author summarizes it as below:

> *We call elements (sections of the text–morphemes or morpheme sequences) equivalent to each other if they occur in the environment of (other) identical or equivalent elements* [emphasis added]. Each set of mutually equivalent elements is called an equivalence class. Each successive sentence of the text is then represented as a sequence of equivalence classes, namely those to which its various sections belong. We thus obtain for the whole text a double array, the horizontal axis representing the equivalence classes contained in one sentence, and the vertical axis representing successive sentences. *This is a tabular arrangement not of sentence structures (subjects, verbs, and the like), but of the patterned occurrence of the equivalence classes through the text* [emphasis added]. (Harris, 1952, pp. 9-10)

So briefly, the method collects elements that evaluate in the same environment in a sentence and categorizes them as members of the same equivalence class (Harris, 1952, pp. 29-30). To do so, one needs to divide sentences in several intervals – adjectival and/or verbal. Finally, the sequence of intervals is analysed according to the distribution of equivalence classes which reveals different patterns of occurrences (Harris, 1952, p. 30). In my concrete case, I will apply this procedure to speeches pronounced by executive leaders of different types of countries – the leading member, the contributing member and the opposing member – to compare them between themselves and through time. In regard to the chronological comparison, one may criticize it by saying that the countries compared will not be the same through time and cases but only supposedly the same "type". Even if it sets up a certain limit for the chronological comparison, I think chosen countries are emblematic members of disagreements about the out-of-area problem for each case. It minimizes the effect of a potential limitation. On the more technical side, I realize the predicate analysis in a semi-automated manner through the Stanford CoreNLP toolkit (Manning et al., 2014). This pipeline software is designed for annotation of the raw text put through the machine given the information that the user wants to have (Manning et al., 2014, p. 55). I used for my part the "parses" feature to see the full syntactic analysis of the text: it provides all the basic and enhanced dependencies in sentences (Manning et al., 2014, p. 58). I putted all texts through the machine – paragraph per paragraph – and after identifying all noun phrases, I started to write down all discursive subjects in a sentence accompanied by its adjectival and verbal predicates. Then, I selected some key discursive subjects[28] in raw texts for my dissertation which are the following[29]: NATO, I – the speaker – , speaker's country, the coalition, and Europe. Once these elements identified, I regrouped them with their predicates and organized equivalence classes which I summarized in a different table for each country. The **Table 2** below summarizes the methodology adopted for my dissertation in broad outline.

---

[28] Based on their recurrence rate in a given corpus data for a speaker.
[29] These were not all available for all speakers, but it is the general template that I used.

Table 2 The general methodology of the dissertation

	Complement	*Cases*		
Out-of-area norm	**During late-Cold War (1980-1991)**	**Bosnian war case (1992-1995)**	**Iraq war case (2003-2011)**	**Libyan war case (2011)**
Actors	The U.S. and NATO	*The U.S.* (leading member), *Germany* (contributing member), *Greece* (opposing member) and NATO	*The U.K.* (leading member), *Spain* (contributing member), *Canada* (opposing member) and NATO	*France* (leading member), *Turkey* (contributing member), *Czech Republic* (opposing member) and NATO
Unit of observation	Bureaucrats' documents	Executive leaders' and SGs's speeches		
Sources	Historical documents (Memoranda, press statements and a special article)	Corpus of paragraphs from speeches		
Method	Archival analysis	Predicate analysis (Core NLP)		

## V)	The evolution of the norm in the Alliance

In this chapter, I present the results of my research and provide a discussion of them. I make completely available all the data and related materials I used (see the **"Data Availability"** section).

5.1) During the late-Cold War (1980–1991)

The project of changing the out-of-area norm in NATO was already in the agenda of the U.S. from the 1980s, only waiting for the right moment to be revived in debates (Liland, 1999, pp. 113-126; Stuart & Tow, 1990, pp. 317-320). Moreover, the Americans were also doing lobbying activities in the backstage with some member countries in order to see who may support them or not during a potential revival of the out-of-area norm change process. I show in this section, through memoranda and other documents, how this idea was occupying the minds of the U.S. bureaucrats and soldiers who were trying to guess what might be the reaction of others if they reanimate the debate of the norm change.

The U.S. strategic departments' positions on a potential out-of-area norm change process were rather mixed but, in any case, cautious.

The first document about the U.S. is a series of paper written by the DOS, reviewed by the National Security Council ('**NSC**'), and prepared by the Senior Interagency Group No. 17 under the supervision of the Executive Secretary L. Paul Bremer III (1982b). It is entitled "NATO Summit Preparations", dating from 1 March 1982. The document is collected from the CIA archives. Its main purpose is to prepare relevant department bureaucrats for the upcoming NATO Council meeting held during June in Bonn. The meeting resulted in a declaration named "Peace in Freedom". The main topics that the member countries had in mind during these months were: greater Soviet restraint, development of East-West relationship, arms control, human rights issues and the Helsinki Final Act. The document is addressed to Ms Nancy Bearg Dyke from the Office of the Vice-President ('**OVP**'), Mr Michael O. Wheeler from the NSC, Colonel John Stanford from the United States Department of Defense ('**DOD**'), Lieutenant Colonel Edward Bucknell from the Joint Chiefs of Staff ('**JCS**'), Mr David Pickford from the Treasury, and Mr Joseph Presel from the Arms Control and Disarmament Agency ('**ACDA**'). It contains an agenda, a discussion paper, a work programme, and the calendar of relevant events. Amongst these parts, the discussion paper entitled "The NATO Summit: An Atlantic Agenda for the 1980's" is very interesting for the subject of this dissertation. In this paper, some general advice and guidelines are given by the experts. It is emphasized that the Summit will be "a forum which focuses major attention on the leadership of the Alliance" and "a Presidential show" (Bremer, 1982b, p. 1). The experts advise "the U.S. emerge from it as the confident leader of a unified Alliance" (Bremer, 1982b, p. 1). They acknowledge the important disagreements existing between members on the areas of economic, defence, and foreign policy matters. For that reason, they suggest focusing on the subjects for which there is a consensus, in order to build a strong and united image of NATO vis-à-vis the exterior world (Bremer, 1982b, p. 1). They wish the following outcomes from the summit for the U.S.: global restraint and responsibility underlined as the main purpose of NATO, lay down of NATO's vision for the 1980s based on the new challenges and opportunities, and conventional defence issues being one of the major dossiers of the Summit (Bremer, 1982b, pp. 1-2). Inside the building blocks of political issues prepared for the summit, there is a talking point entitled "Out-Of-Area Issues and Global Concerns". The following passage from the point summarizes perfectly the U.S. vision about the out-of-area norm status before the Summit:

> [...] *we will want explicit recognition by the Summit of this threat* [emphasis added]. Specifically, we should seek language in the Summit declaration endorsing individual or collective Alliance efforts which contribute to out-of-area stability and to Western and regional security. We should continue to nudge the Allies on the specific areas where we have sought increased cooperation from them. *However, we also wish to avoid divisive debate at the Summit on issues where we continue to have important differences—for example, the Arab-Israeli dispute, El Salvador and Libya* [emphasis added]. (Bremer, 1982b, p. 3)

We can easily assess that the U.S. wanted at least a verbal recognition of new threats to the Alliance by the Council and its members. One should also keep in mind that the U.S. cleverly linked out-of-area threats to the Soviet one through the Soviet-Afghan war during the Summit, in order to get more support for its wish of out-of-area issues' inclusion in the agenda (Bremer, 1982b, p. 3). Simultaneously, they were also strategic by being careful to not to mention controversial problems which may potentially break the consensus already reached on the recognition point. Through this document, we see how the U.S. proceeded step by step to set up the out-of-area problematic in member countries' minds before initiating the norm change once again.

The second document is a top-secret memorandum written by the DOS and prepared again by L. Paul Bremer III (1982a). It is entitled "Interagency Review Group Meeting on NSSD 1-

82, U.S. National Security Strategy", dating from 11 March 1982. It is collected from the CIA archives. It aims to share the vision of the interagency group on the National Security Studies Directives ('**NSSD**') 1-82 with the President's Office and other relevant departments. It is part of the preparations for the upcoming NATO Council meeting in June 1982. The document is addressed to Mr William P. Clark from the White House, Colonel John Stanford from the Office of the Secretary of Defense ('**OSD**'), and Lieutenant Colonel Edward Bucknell from the JCS. The content is as follows: a discussion paper on the role of the allies with a summary, and two issues papers (Bremer, 1982a). In the "Roles of Allies and Others", the memorandum reveals the divergence of points of view in the interagency group regarding whether or not the U.S. should ask Europe's assistance for out-of-area Soviet threats and if yes, in which ways (Bremer, 1982a, p. 1). Two opinions are presented in the memorandum with their own justification. The first one defends the idea of European participation in the resolution of out-of-area problems through the encouragement of countries who can and have the willingness to do so. Here they mostly refer to the U.K. and France who may contribute by allocating their marginal defence resources towards potential out-of-area operations (Bremer, 1982a, p. 1). The tenants of this position rely on several arguments to defend their idea, which are summed up in the following paragraph:

> Some believe that, if forthcoming, Allied contributions could add both to deterrence and warfighting capabilities on a political (European involvement/Alliance cohesion) as well as military level. […] *Even if European contributions were small, the solidarity of US-European opposition would indicate to the Soviets that they could not seek to outflank the Alliance militarily or divide the Alliance politically by attacks outside the Treaty area* [emphasis added]. […] Moreover, those Europeans who could contribute could be more easily encouraged to devote additional resources for defense in areas of greater marginal return, e.g., dual-use European/SWA security forces. (Bremer, 1982a, p. 13)

As apparent in their justification, the defendants of this position mainly value the symbolic contribution of Europe to out-of-area problems for solidarity purposes. In doing so, NATO could legitimately claim to unity against the Soviet Union. It also adds more legitimacy to potential operational moves compared to a U.S. alone or ad hoc coalition manoeuvres. It is interesting to see once again the emphasize of Soviet origins in out-of-area problems threatening the Alliance. On the other side, the second camp defends the idea of not insisting on the European participation in out-of-area operations. They justify their position by two main arguments:

> Given the limited forces likely to be made available by contributing Allies, the technical/operational problems of planning for coalition warfare appear to some to outweigh the potential benefits of a coalition strategy. […] In addition, those who argue for this option submit that additional European resource allocations are more needed in Europe than SWA and that they are more likely to be encouraged for political reasons for missions tied exclusively to Europe. (Bremer, 1982a, p. 13)

The first point is in itself farsighted because operational planning complications between member allies were effectively an issue during NATO's intervention in Bosnia and Kosovo. By this idea, they implicitly promote ad hoc coalitions of the willing if needed rather than operations under NATO's banner with extensive member participation. The second point also seems logical: European countries could only be persuaded for potential out-of-area operations directly linked to their geographical sphere. Hence, it does not make sense to push them for out-of-area operations since more resources are needed in Europe in any case. To sum up, we can see in this memorandum that governmental and military actors in the U.S. took into account all kinds of possibilities for out-of-area implication seriously. They were not blind on alternative options before reanimating the debate over the norm change.

Then, there is an interesting article written by an ancient government official Charles Waterman (1985) entitled "US strategic thinkers debate pros and cons of using 'proxy states'". The document comes from the CIA archives. It discusses whether or not the U.S. should use proxy states, published in the Christian Science Monitor on 3 September 1985. The publication date is after the meeting of the Defence Planning Committee in May and just before the Brussels summit of NATO heads of states in November. The article consists of several points which are: a summary on how the Soviet Union used and continues to use proxy states, how the U.S. could do the same, categories of potential cooperative "proxy" forces and potential disadvantages of using this strategy (Waterman, 1985). The categories of "cooperative forces" are namely:

> States which would be available to intervene in target areas distant from their own borders. […] States which would agree to assume security responsibility for a neighbouring region, and engage in contingency planning with the US for prospective intervention. […] States willing to sustain a pro-Western insurgency in a bordering country. […] Insurgents willing to engage in insurrection against a state hostile to the West. (Waterman, 1985, p. 1)

Since the U.S. did not succeed in convincing sufficient number of allied member countries of the necessity to change the out-of-area norm, policy experts commenced to look for alternative solutions against extraterritorial threats. The main point of opposition from NATO members that the U.S. consulted was the nonsense of intervening in issues not directly threatening their territory. They also feared to see NATO becoming a global policeman. This alternative solution of "proxy states" is nonetheless not perfect: the political price of a long insurrection could be high as seen in Nicaraguan contras case (Waterman, 1985, p. 1).

There is another secret memorandum written by an anonymous Acting National Intelligence Officer for Europe (NIC, 1986) on June 19, entitled "The European Allies' View of the Third World and the Reagan Doctrine". It comes from the CIA archives. It is destined to the Director and Deputy Director of Central Intelligence and discusses the repercussions of the Reagan Doctrine on the European allies' minds in general terms. The document dates of few months after the explosion at Chernobyl in April which underlined the appearance of threats in different nature: national borders are no longer a protective barrier. Moreover, in May of the same year, the ministerial meeting of the NAC issued a statement inviting the Soviet Union to cooperate with NATO to promote peace and security in the World. In this context, the Reagan Doctrine is an important factor and the memorandum consists of seven points: executive summary, historical trends of the differences, differences in policy priorities, trend to see the U.S. and Soviet Union foreign policy as similar, favourable trends, specificity of favourable trends, and categories of intelligence support for the Reagan Doctrine in Europe (NIC, 1986, pp. 1-3). To be brief, the document concludes that Europe does not agree with the U.S. vision of confronting the Soviet Union outside of the Atlantic territory, meaning the Third World. This is due to different perceptions of the Soviet Union and different national interests concerning the foreign policy. One of the main concerns is the possibility of the Reagan Doctrine to push for out-of-area operations using NATO forces. More concretely, their perception of out-of-area operations is summarized by the author as follows:

> they worry that US actions against Soviet clients and associates in the Third World areas could raise East-West tensions, adversely affect their economic interests in the Third World, lead to terrorist retaliation in Europe and, *at the extreme, produce a Soviet-US confrontation that might transcend the Third World* [emphasis added]. (NIC, 1986, p. 2)

Thus, the source of their fear regarding the conduct of out-of-area operations is the potential Soviet reaction. The main obstacle for the U.S. to convince the European allies of the norm change's necessity is then the presence of the Cold War and the Soviet Union. This is why the project of a new norm was in latent mode during the Cold War, waiting for the right moment to be reinserted in the agenda.

Another memorandum prepared by the CIA (1986) on July 22 entitled "Western Europe-United States: Differences over policy towards Libya Highlight Deeper Splits within the Alliance" shed light on the reasons of European reluctance concerning a potential out-of-area norm change. Being from the CIA archives once again, it shows the suppositional conclusions about European divergence with the U.S. on the purpose and role of the Atlantic Alliance (CIA, 1986, p. 1). The preparation of this document is not independent from the U.S. attacks on Tripoli and Benghazi in April of the same year, as a move against terrorist attacks originated from Libya. At that time, Europe strongly disapproved this attitude. The memorandum is distributed to a dozen representatives from relevant departments in the U.S. and contains several points which are: difference of vision regarding the terrorist problem, differences over the role and purpose of NATO, differences over military tactics, and the implications for the U.S. (CIA, 1986, pp. 3-8). The general message is that the Libyan disagreement is only one example of a bigger divergence over out-of-area issues inside NATO. The memorandum assumes that it would probably repeat itself (CIA, 1986, p. 2). Once more, the U.S. and the Europeans disagreed because "the West Europeans insist that the Alliance's objective is to safeguard Western Europe's security–not to stand up for democratic values and Western interests in other parts of the world" (CIA, 1986, p. 4). The fear of NATO's mandate extension on the European camp faces us again in this document, which was the main reason for its reluctance to an out-of-area norm change. This is, of course, eminently linked to the Cold War and Soviet Union presence in the international system.

There are finally two other very important memoranda. The first one is written by the Acting Assistant Secretary for Legislative and Intergovernmental Affairs Betsy R. Warren (1987) from the DOS. The title is "DOD and State draught reports on H.R. 2805, concerning the establishment of a commission to foster more cooperative planning and response by our NATO and Asian allies to out-of-area threats to Western Security interests". It dates from 20 August 1987 and comes from the CIA archives. The letter is destined to Doug Bereuter from the House of Representatives and concerns the opinion of the DOS on the bill about the creation of coordination commission on out-of-area issues affecting the Western Alliance (Warren, 1987, p. 1). The context is very loaded for the Alliance at that time. After the UNSC resolution 598 on the 20th of July inviting Iran and Iraq to end the conflict and return to pre-war boundaries, some NATO member countries decided to launch joint operations for protecting the oil tankers' traffic. The Alliance also celebrated the 20th anniversary of the Harmel report this year. The response of Warren to Bereuter consists of several main points which are regrouped in the following sub-sections: changed global context, necessity of confronting out-of-area issues, nature of these threats and difficulties in addressing them, opinion on the utility of the commission, already existing structure to deal with out-of-area issues, the U.S. individual initiatives, implementing decisions about the out-of-area issues, Persian Gulf problem example, and the conclusion (Warren, 1987, pp. 1-4). First, Warren recognizes the seriousness of new threats to the Western Alliance: indeed, these threats were none existent when NATO was established and consequently it should adopt to meet them. According to him, for an approach to be effective against these new dangers, it should rely on three crucial elements: "consensus among interested allies on how to best address out-of-area issues, proper machinery to coordinate allied policy, and the means to pursue whatever response or action is decided upon" (Warren, 1987, p. 1). Concerning the first point, he says that the early step of problem identification is not challenging but allied members rarely agree on if the problem should be dealt with and if yes in which ways. He gives the example of international terrorism to illustrate the divergences between allies. He supposes that the coordination commission may have a utility in building the consensus of this first step. Nevertheless, he also urges the representatives of potential risks that this type of commission hold: members can just insist on their differences that they already mentioned in other platforms in NATO or, even worse, they can create new disagreements because of the extensive meetings. For the second point, he relates all the other already existing consulting structures in which out-of-area issues are discussed (Warren, 1987, p. 2). Outside of NATO and bilateral exchanges, there are the press, international academic circles, and the UNSC in which out-of-area problems are discussed and taken into consideration seriously. Inside NATO[30], there are the NAC and the DPC as frameworks for regular consultations on existing and emerging out-of-area problems. On the other hand, he finds more effective the individual American bilateral and multilateral initiatives with other countries in

---

[30] For extra information on the consulting process about out-of-area issues in NATO during the Cold War, please see (Stuart & Tow, 1990, p. 321).

order to create out-of-area consensus. In doing so, the U.S. can choose its partners depending on their level of expertise and their acquaintance with the U.S. Finally, on the point of policy implementation, he thinks that it would work better if the U.S. cooperates only with the countries who have the resources ready to be used in missions effectively (Warren, 1987, p. 3). He gives the example of the Persian Gulf operations in Iran-Iraq war to illustrate his point. He argues that the commission could not add anything supplementary to this procedure. To summarize, the opinion of the DOS on a coordination commission is negative because:

> the present system for allied out-of-area policy coordination meets our key requirements. While there are evident merits to the Allied Commission for out-of-area issues proposed in your recent legislation, *it is difficult for us to see how this proposal, if put into effect, would overcome already existing problems* [emphasis added]. (Warren, 1987, p. 3)

So, according to Warren, if member countries already disagree elsewhere they would not agree on this commission structure just because it is a different structure.

The second memorandum is written by the National Intelligence Officer for General Purpose Forces Major General Larry D. Budge (1987), from the National Intelligence Council ('**NIC**'). It is entitled "Allied Commission on Out-of-Area issues Act, H.R. 2805", dating from September 10. It is once more from the CIA archives. It is a response destined to the legislation division of the Office of Congressional Affairs and concerns this time the opinion of the NIC on the famous bill. Budge produces a short but very meaningful response. He reminds that NATO is a successful alliance because it is created against a common threat which is the Soviet Union. Given the diversified nature of the out-of-area problems together with the divergent national perceptions and interests, he thinks that the Commission would not be able to generate the necessary consensus to act on these problems (Budge, 1987, p. 1). Consequently, the NIC's opinion about the bill is negative too.

On the side of other NATO member countries, reactions to a potential change were rather negative or only verbally supportive up to a certain level.

Let's start with a secret memorandum written by the director of European and NATO Affairs, United States Air Force's ('**USAF**') major general Richard C. Bowman (1981), entitled "Bilateral Meeting with the Turks". The document is collected from the CIA archives. It is a record of the meeting that the Americans had with their Turkish counterparts in the Conference room number 7 of the NATO HQ on 15 May 1981. It is held two days after the general meetings of the DPC, having in mind instabilities in Poland and a potential Soviet intervention in this country. Participants were, on the U.S. side: Secretary of Defense Weinberger, Ambassador W. Tapley Bennett, Dr Fred C. Ikle, General Richard C. Bowman, and Brigadier General Carl Smith. On the Turkish side, they were: The Ministry of Defence Haluk Bayülken and other members of the delegation. Apparently, the meeting consisted of four "confidential" and two "secret" points. The confidential points are: Delivery of Military assistance material, military assistance in the new budget, M-48 Tank Modernization, and Military Assistance Planning (Bowman, 1981, pp. 1-2). More interesting for this dissertation, the secret points are as follows: Turkish Air Force Spare Parts and Turkish Assistance to the U.S. in out-of-area crises (Bowman, 1981, pp. 1-2). According to the memorandum, the Turkish Ministry of Defence assured the Americans of Turkey's full support in any potential out-of-area crises. In his words, Bowman recapitulates this support by:

> Bayülken said Turkey would do whatever was necessary when the chips were down. [...] Weinberger agreed that the Turkish forces were very important for the stability of the area and said that the U.S. appreciated their quality. *Bayülken added that it would be very important to have a NATO umbrella for out-of-area actions* [emphasis added]. (Bowman, 1981, p. 2)

As we can see, at that time already, Turkey shown its support for the out-of-area norm change and the creation of a structure inside the Alliance to deal with these problems. The U.S. on its side noted this support as the last and most important secret point in a memorandum. This reveals the importance that the U.S. accorded to the support of other NATO members before re-initiating the norm change. The document is a manifestation of the American lobbying in the backstage for the creation of a consensus on the necessity to reform the old out-of-area norm.

Next, there is a top-secret memorandum of conversation written by USAF's Brigadier General and the Deputy Assistant Secretary of Defense Europe/NATO Policy John R. Lasater (1982). The document is collected from the Office of the Historian DOS archives (Lasater, 1982). It is a record of the meeting that the Americans had with their British counterparts concerning the Falklands war at the NATO HQ on 6 May 1982 from 8 to 8:30 a.m. The date corresponds to the start of the DPC meetings in which consultation on effect of out-of-area deployments – mainly illustrated by the Falklands war – was an important subject. Participants were, on the U.S. side: Secretary Weinberger, Ambassador Bennett, Defence Advisor Legere, General Smith, and General Lasater (Lasater, 1982, p. 484). On the British side, participants were: Ministry of Defence Nott, Ambassador Graham, and Mr Hastie-Smith (Lasater, 1982, p. 484). The conversation consisted of several points such as the actual situation in the Falklands, ongoing diplomatic initiatives, assistance needs on the U.K. side and finally out-of-area threats to NATO (Lasater, 1982, pp. 484-486). The last point consists of one of the most explicit paragraphs amongst all documents concerning the bargain over the out-of-area norm, which I relate here without cutting it:

> SecDef raised the issue of out-of-area threats to NATO's interest and the requirement for NATO committed forces to be utilized for contingencies in other parts of the world. The Falklands crisis was indeed just such an example and he asked MOD Nott's views on using the current crisis to underscore that need. MOD Nott responded that he had no objections but would caution against the United States making the case that Europe was more dependent on mid-East oil than was the United States. Ambassador Graham added that one must keep in mind when making a case for Southwest Asia as a threat to NATO that we bear in mind that we also open the doors to the European nations demanding the right to be consulted and to approve of all deployments outside the NATO area. *ASD Perle inquired whether or [Page 486] not in the British view it would not be possible to draft a simple and straightforward statement recognizing threats to NATO's interest and the need to plan to meet those threats* [emphasis added]. *The British side did not respond* [emphasis added]. (Lasater, 1982, pp. 485-486)

We read in this script how the U.S. opportunistically seized the occasion of the Falklands war to see whether it can convince the British to support them for a potential out-of-area norm change in NATO. They naturally thought that since the U.K. itself went out-of-area – experienced the difficulty to be alone – and would appreciate a more extensive support from the Atlantic Alliance, it could support a norm change at least for the future. To their surprise, the British position on this issue was neutral considering their reaction. Furthermore, they urged the U.S. of a potential NATO's mandate extension if the possibility is given to members to bring all out-of-area deployments for discussion in the Council. The U.S. did not get the support it waited and wanted from the U.K. at that time. It shows again the lobbying in the backstage of the Americans and how they value the support of other allied members without power consideration, given the consensual decision-making nature of NATO.

On the side of the NATO bureaucracy, the reaction to a potential change agenda was clearly negative.

The most blatant document published by the Alliance during the Cold War about out-of-area issues is the "Document on Integrated NATO Defense" released on 10 June 1982 in Bonn by the NATO Press Service (1982). It is from the NATO online archives. The document aims to declare the Alliance's integrated defence structure programme for the upcoming ten years. It is published after the Summit meeting held in Bonn with the participation of heads of states and governments. The meeting was an occasion to set up the points for NATO's adaptation to the changing international security context. The document consists of five main points which are: fulfilment of NATO Force Goals, implementing measures of the Long-Term Defence Programme, improvement of the NATO planning procedure, resorting to emerging technologies, and consultations about out-of-area issues (NATO, 1982, pp. 1-2). The last point is naturally the most relevant for my dissertation. The Alliance's integrated defence structure recognizes the negative impact that out-of-area problems might have on the treaty area.

Therefore, it attaches great importance to the inside consultation process of NATO to identify the problems on a common basis. Nevertheless, regarding the actions to be taken, it makes the following interesting remark which is:

> Recognising that the policies which nations adopt in this field are a matter for national decision, we agree to examine collectively in the appropriate NATO bodies the requirements which may arise for the defence of the NATO area as a result of deployments by individual member states outside that area. Steps which may be taken by individual Allies in the light of such consultations to facilitate possible military deployments beyond the NATO area can represent an important contribution to Western security. (NATO, 1982, p. 2)

As apparent in the passage *supra*, NATO integrated defence structure body had no intention to change the out-of-area norm in the Alliance. For them, the most that NATO can do is to provide a consultation platform for member States and take precautions inside the area when a member nation decides to move some parts of its troops out-of-area. This document shows that NATO member countries' heads of states and governments agree on the following point: The Alliance shall not be directly involved in out-of-area problems and must concentrate on its core defence mission.

To sum up, the U.S. tentative to reanimate the change process of the out-of-area norm in NATO during the late-Cold War was not successful. The U.S. acted strategically by not mentioning controversial topics and linking out-of-area problems to the greater Soviet one. Despite the fact that it had the support of some member countries (e.g., Turkey), it was not sufficient to initiate a norm change. Interestingly, the support came from a country at the border of the NATO treaty area and who had the greatest risk to be exposed to out-of-area problems.[31] On the other hand, the U.K. preferred to remain neutral and silent on this subject even if they did not reject this possibility completely. The European countries opposed a change in the out-of-area norm in NATO at that period because of three main reasons: The Cold War context and

---

[31] For more information on this point, you can for instance have a look at Winrow (1993).

the danger of escalation due to an intervention in the Third World, the presence of the Soviet Union who may retaliate in Europe because of NATO's out-of-area activities and the unnecessity of the Alliance's mandate extension whose main purpose is to defend the treaty area. Conscious of these concerns, the U.S. also looked for some alternative solutions such as using proxy states or the creation of coordination commission on out-of-area issues containing non-NATO member allied countries (e.g., Japan). These initiatives were all let down because of complications discussed above. One should keep in mind that not all actors in the U.S. were favourable to a norm change in the Western Alliance anyway. Apart from the executive power branch, most of the other departments underlined their preference of the U.S. individual bilateral and multilateral initiatives in these issues. So, the U.S. did not bring back the out-of-area norm change subject in NATO's agenda until the end of the Cold War. In the following sections, we are going to see how the change process started and evolved over twenty years always with the U.S. pushing first. In the absence of a common threat and without the Cold War context, I am going to show if the "mandate extension" counter-argument had a value in the opposing countries' discourse to the norm change.

5.2) The Bosnian War case (1992–1995)

After the Cold War, the out-of-area norm in NATO began to change in the discourse and practices of the member countries. Without doubt, the dissolution of the Soviet Union played the major role in this change. In a globalized and unipolar world, the Alliance found different opportunities to expand its mandate and intervene in problematic cases. As we can see in the map **below**, in 2014 NATO was for instance very active in out-of-area and even in "out-of-continent" whether through peacekeeping, peace building, humanitarian assistance, training, military intervention, etc. (Stratfor, 2014).

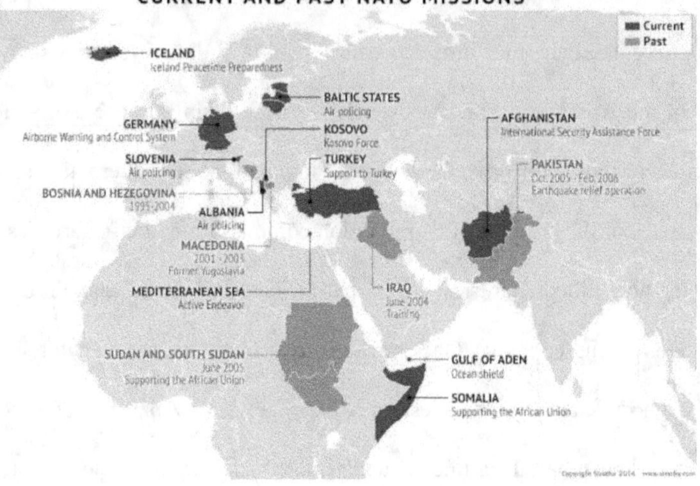

Figure 1 The map of NATO missions in 2014

Source: Stratfor (2014)

The Bosnian War was the first major out-of-area intervention that NATO realized since its existence. It was an armed conflict that took place in Bosnia. The war mainly opposed the armed forces of the Republic of Bosnia and Herzegovina with those of Republika Srpska and Herzeg-Bosnia. It happened in the context of the Yugoslavia breakup. After the referendum on independence, the Bosnia and Herzegovina declared its independence. It led to the rejection of it by the Serbs and Croats and the beginning of an ethnic conflict characterized with several war crimes (e.g., Siege of Sarajevo, Srebrenica massacre, etc.) (ICTY, 2017).[32] Following the Srebrenica and Markale massacres, NATO decided to intervene[33] in 1995 through air strikes under the name "Operation Deliberate Force" targeting strategic military positions of Republika Srpska army. This intervention was crucial in ending the conflict: it resulted in the Dayton Agreement on 21 November 1995 (ICTY, 2017). Besides the fact that NATO conducted air strikes or provided air support only in request of the UN resolutions, important disagreements occurred between member countries because of this issue. The tension was mainly about the

---

[32] The International Criminal Tribunal for the former Yugoslavia ('**ICTY**').
[33] Following subsequent UN resolutions as well.

timing and the way in which air power of NATO should be used, confronting the U.S. to the Western European countries. Given the U.S. did not have any ground troops in Bosnia but was insisting for air strikes while the Europeans did have ground troops amplified this tension, as we are going to see in more details below.

The U.S. is labelled as a "leading member" for the Bosnian War case because from the beginning of the conflict until its end, it was the country who contributed the most to all military, political and social initiatives to resolve the problem. For instance, the U.S. insisted for a long time for the removal of arms embargo in Bosnia which was opposed by the European allies (Branch, 2009). As the refusal persisted, the U.S. notwithstanding smuggled weapons to Bosnia via back channels and turned blind eye to other countries who also did the same (e.g., Iran, Pakistan, Turkey, etc.). The speaker I chose is Bill Clinton: he is the 42nd President of the U.S. and *de jure* leader of the executive power branch at that time. The speech corpus for this speaker contains extracts from six speeches from 1994 to 1996 (Clinton, 1994a, 1994b, 1994c, 1994d, 1995a, 1996a). The time frame corresponds to one year before the launch of the "Operation Deliberate Force" and one year after the end of the war. There are three key discursive subjects emerging from the paragraphs: NATO, the U.S. and Yugoslavia. The NATO cluster contains 27 equivalent classes, the U.S. one contains 52, and the Yugoslavia subject contains 12. The adjectival and verbal attributes are mixed. I am going to analyse the results cluster by cluster while only looking into the most relevant equivalence classes when there are a lot of predicates, in light of the subject of my dissertation.

The NATO cluster in Bill Clinton's speeches is portrayed as a very active and unique military alliance. NATO "must confront the destabilizing consequences" (Clinton, 1994d) according to Clinton: the need for change is underlined without hesitation. At the same time, NATO is not alone, or the change cannot be accomplished by itself only: because NATO is "acting out of area pursuant to UN authority" (Clinton, 1994a). A change in some SOPs does not mean that every procedure is relinquished in the Alliance: in fact, decisions are still made through consensus and any action "requires the common agreement of our NATO allies" (Clinton, 1994a) recognizes Clinton. The Alliance's readiness to intervene in the Bosnian War is explicitly proclaimed by the U.S. president: NATO is ready to conduct air strikes if necessary. The speaker also refers to adjectival predicates to narrate the merits of NATO by evoking adjectives such as "greatest", "powerful" and says that it is the unique military power which has the possibility to end the conflict in Bosnia. He concedes that it is the first time NATO goes out-of-area and change its position from a defensive to an offensive one. On the other hand, it is thanks to NATO's air strikes that Bosnian Serbs returned to the negotiation table and peace is established in the country. Therefore, NATO's new role in the changing security context is utile and undeniable.

The U.S. cluster in the speaker's speeches is described as an active, cooperative and leading ally in NATO. Clinton remarks the multivariate relationships of his country with other actors concerning the Bosnian War: the U.S. is "ready to help NATO" (Clinton, 1994d), wants to give a chance to UN, and works constructively with other members of the Western Alliance. The U.S. welcomes an increased contribution to the burden-sharing in NATO by other allies. This cooperation idea does not only concern the European countries but all kinds of allies from the Eastern European countries to Russia. By this attitude, the U.S. laid the foundation of the PfP and NATO-Russia Council at that time. The president also argues that his country is very active regarding the Bosnian conflict and done a lot of things for peace. The U.S. broke the siege of Sarajevo, ended the massacre, prevented the spread of the conflict and the increase of refugees' flows, brought back the belligerents to the negotiation table, etc. Finally, the headship characteristic of the U.S. is emphasized several times by the president. The U.S. leadership in the world is needed for everyone as he says. He relates all the facts justifying the benefits of American leadership such as the U.S. participation in the WWII, the Marshall Plan, the creation of NATO, etc. In this framework, the U.S. also took the management of the Bosnian War by leading the air strikes and economic sanctions and being the "primary broker of the peace agreement" (Clinton, 1995a). More interesting for this dissertation, in Clinton's speeches the U.S. is also portrayed as the leading country in NATO. The U.S. is the country who shows the utility of NATO to everyone in the new century, builds a "new NATO for a new era" (Clinton, 1996a), is adapting the Alliance with new missions, opening its doors to Eastern European countries and Russia, concentrates on few and flexible forces while preserving core NATO functions, and will continue to take the lead in the Western Alliance. The U.S. wants a change and leads it.

The Yugoslavia discursive subject is narrated as a problematic European country that needs help. According to Clinton, the country is characterized by economic and ethnic problems. It is an ally at the centre of Europe and a neighbour of "fragile new democracies" (Clinton, 1995a). The speaker also labels this subject as needing help: the conflictual situation in the region should be resolved through negotiated solutions. Therefore, these attributes given by the speaker implicitly justify the first NATO out-of-area intervention in this region.

To epitomize, the U.S. position about the out-of-area norm change is very clear: NATO is an active and skilful Alliance which needs to meet the new emerging threats wherever they come. The U.S. in this change process is the leading country who wants the adaptation of the Alliance while also keeping the core functions. The U.S. "helps" NATO too by its cooperative and bridge-building attitude with external actors to the Western Alliance. The out-of-area intervention in Bosnia is justified by the European and proximate nature of the conflict. Interestingly, since it is the earlier steps of the norm change process, the U.S. executive resorts to the geographical proximity argument of the problem in order to persuade others of the intervention's legitimacy.

I label Germany as the "contributing member" in the Bosnian War case owing to its supports to bring peace back in this region at all steps of the conflict and even after the Dayton Agreement. It is one of the rare countries who endorsed a potential lift of the UN arms embargo (Branch, 2009, p. 31). Germany also reused its air force for the first time since the end of the WWII during the "Operation Deliberate Force". The speaker for this country is Helmut Kohl: he was the Chancellor of Germany at that time. The corpus for him consists of extracts from nine speeches held from 1992 to 1996 (Clinton, 1993, 1994e, 1995b, 1995c, 1996b; Kohl, 1992, 1994, 1996a, 1996b).[34] His first speech is held three days before the start of the Bosnian War. For the purpose of enhanced comparability between discourses and given the German grammar and sentence structure's uniqueness, I personally translated into English the passages extracted from the following four speeches: Kohl (1992, 1994, 1996a, 1996b). There are again three key discursive subjects which emerge from the predicate analysis: NATO, Germany and Yugoslavia. The NATO subject is composed of 19 equivalent classes, Germany contains 13, and Yugoslavia cluster contains two.

The NATO subject in Chancellor's speeches is designated as indispensable, active and in transformation for new mandates. Its indispensability is underlined by several adjectival and verbal predicates: it is a guarantee for Europe's future, common security and peace. More than a military alliance, it is also a union of free and democratic nations, a community of values and ideas. NATO is also very active might this be specifically for the Bosnian War case or other issues. The Alliance is "determined to act" (Kohl, 1996b) and "secure peace in this region" (Kohl, 1996a). Finally, Kohl recognizes the necessity of NATO's change in order to adapt itself to the new security context in which it has "a role to play" (Clinton, 1996b). It needs to be able to "tackle new challenges" (Kohl, 1996b) with new structures. It should enlarge its protection domain to the "peoples of the world" (Clinton, 1996b). After the collapse of communism,

---

[34] The speeches authored "Clinton" are in fact joint press conferences of both leaders, held in the U.S.

NATO should be the key organization for the stabilization of the whole European continent. According to the Chancellor, NATO is "very much in business".

The "Germany" cluster in the extracts is represented as conscious of its responsibilities and ready to play an active role in the Bosnian War. The Chancellor says that Germany knows "the growing expectations of the international community" (Kohl, 1996b) and is ready to contribute. The country "must" do something but at the same time it must be "careful" not to overlap its limits. It is "happy" to contribute to securing peace in Europe. The country is also labelled as being in agreement with the U.S. and thinks that NATO should fulfil its role regarding the Bosnian War. Thus, the "Germany" discursive subject has all the characteristics of a contributing member to a NATO mission. The Yugoslavia cluster is simply related as a very tragic conflict which revealed the limits and fragilities of the European security.

To sum up, Germany also expresses a positive opinion about the out-of-area norm change in NATO: even though its position is not clear enough as in the U.S. case, Kohl tacitly recognizes and understands NATO's transformation in order to adapt to the new context. Germany knows perfectly its role in this change process and is ready to contribute as necessary on the ground as well as on the table. The intervention in Bosnia is justified by the gravity of the situation. Since the conflict date corresponds to just several years after the German reunification, one should keep in mind that the German attitude is naturally more pro-U.S. and cooperative in the Atlantic Alliance.

For this case, Greece is labelled as an "opposing member" due to its reluctance to explicitly support NATO out-of-area missions in the region. During the debates about the potential use of air strikes under the "Operation Deliberate Force" to put an end to the conflict, Greece was the only member who did not support such an action. Moreover, in addition to the support provided by some political factions in Greece to the Republika Srpska, the participation of the Greek Volunteer Guard paramilitaries to the conflict putted the Greek government in a very controversial position (Michas, 2002). The speaker for this country is Andreas Papandreou: he was the prime minister of Greece between 1993 and 1996. The data corpus for this leader contains paragraphs from two speeches held in 1994 (Clinton, 1994f, 1994g). Unfortunately, because of his fragile health and hospitalization in 1995 owing to serious diseases, I was not able to find additional speeches from him on this subject. The date corresponds to one year before the launch of the "Operation Deliberate Force" and extracts from speeches often refer to the opinion of the Greek government on the air strikes possibility. There are three key discursive subjects emerging from the results: NATO, Greece and Yugoslavia. The NATO cluster comprises two equivalent classes, Greece 11, and Yugoslavia three.

The NATO cluster in Papandreou's speeches is narrated as an active and peaceful alliance at the same time. He says NATO is not an enemy for Russia and actively engaged in the Bosnian War by directing an "ultimatum to the Serbs" (Clinton, 1994g).[35] On the other hand, the Yugoslavia subject is invoked as a risky and "tragic" entity. According to him, the war can spread across the region. The content of these clusters is similar to precedent speakers' ones.

The Greece discursive subject is recounted as cooperative but hesitant about the Bosnian War. As stated by the prime minister, Greece acknowledges its part of responsibility in this conflict impacting the region and wants the peace as everyone. Apropos the air strikes, Greece plays it co-operatively by not blocking/vetoing the decision but "express [...] reservations" (Clinton, 1994g). On this point, the vision of Greece is on the opposite of the allied members majority: the country thinks there is "no possible military solution to the problem" (Clinton, 1994g) and the conflict should be resolved by political and diplomatic means. This attitude is different compared to the results of previous predicate analysis relating to the two countries.

In fine, Greece does not have a positive opinion about the out-of-area norm change in NATO: even if the importance of the Alliance is admitted by the speaker, he implicitly

---

[35] From a joint conference at the White House.

disfavours out-of-area interventions by referring to NATO's peaceful nature and the use of political solutions instead of military ones.[36] Greece is nevertheless presented as cooperative meaning that the country does not completely reject the norm change but only discomforted by it. Papandreou illustrates Greece as a country bearing equal responsibility for the conflict and seeking the establishment of a peaceful solution as every other European countries. The tragedy of the Bosnian War is accepted. These results are not independent from the anti-American stance that Papandreou held during his whole political career, especially in military affairs.

The SG of NATO from 1988 to 1994 is Manfred Wörner. From the beginning of the conflict, he was very in favour of a greater role for NATO in the region. The corpus for him is made up of paragraphs from eight speeches held between 1992 and 1993 (Wörner, 1992, 1993a, 1993b, 1993c, 1993d, 1993e, 1993f, 1993g). Once again and regrettably, I was not able to find relevant speeches from the SG for the following years due to his resignation and precocious death in 1994. The time frame corresponds to the start date of the Bosnian War and several months after the launch of the "Operation Deny Flight" by NATO. Two of his speeches (Wörner, 1993b, 1993c) embody paragraphs in French which I kept intact as in their original language: Core NLP supports the French language for dependency parses. In this case, I identified four key discursive subjects in the basic dependencies' results: NATO, the U.S., Yugoslavia and Europe. The NATO subject takes in 49 equivalent classes, the U.S. one, Yugoslavia four, and Europe three.

The U.S. cluster is described as powerful and the main security provider for Europe. Wörner qualifies it as the "garante de la sécurité européenne" (Wörner, 1993b) and therefore underlines the superiority of the American leadership in the Atlantic Alliance. On the other side of the mirror, Europe is qualified as weak and not capable of defending itself by its own means. Wörner explicitly aims the European members of NATO and says that they are "unwilling or

---

[36] Sub-regional implications and geopolitics do certainly also play a role in this position.

unable to assume their responsibilities" (Wörner, 1993g). In parallel to this, he argues that there is an undeniable relationship between the security of European members of NATO and other non-member countries of the *vieux continent*. Without doubt, these predicates refer to the Bosnian War case. The speaker somehow psychologically subordinates the European security and defence to the U.S. strategic leadership. The Yugoslavia discursive subject is depicted as an opportunity for NATO and also a case showing the importance of burden-sharing. The SG sees this case as an occasion for the Alliance to show its "unique potential" and "vitality" for the European security. As an example of out-of-area threat to impact the treaty area, Yugoslavia demonstrates "qu'il importe de partager leadership et responsabilités" (Wörner, 1993c). Compared to previous speakers, the predicates in these extracts for the Yugoslavia cluster are verbal and more directed towards action than only adjectival and qualifying.

The NATO subject in Wörner's speeches is outlined as having new roles, cooperative, active, and an alliance which buried the out-of-area problem. After the Cold War, NATO started to accomplish new missions without hesitation. The cluster has new roles such as "projecting stability", "use of force", "crisis management", "combat operations", "enforcing the embargo", and "peacekeeping" (Wörner, 1993d). Wörner refers to NATO's existing military assets and infrastructure that facilitated the transformation process of the Alliance for new missions. Consequently, NATO's future is directed towards a "modèle d'intégration modulaire" (Wörner, 1993b). Naturally and as it was the case in previous cases above, the Alliance is also categorized as an active organization. It actively contributes to existing missions (e.g., oversight of the no-fly zone in Bosnia, conducting air strikes, using air power, etc.) and is ready to deploy forces on the ground collectively, if necessary. This sustained activity level of the organization whatever the international security context is a proof of its "flexibility" and "pragmatism", in the opinion of the SG. Third, NATO is also portrayed as a cooperative alliance. On the one hand, it cooperates extensively with other international organizations such as the UN and the

Conference on Security and Cooperation in Europe ('**CSCE**'). It provides them political and military support such as the "air power" or "command and control equipment" to the United Nations Protection Force ('**UNPROFOR**'). On the other hand, it wishes to incorporate former countries of the U.S.S.R. into the Atlantic Alliance mechanism through distinct frameworks of relationship. Finally, as maintained by Wörner, NATO seems to have resolved the problem of in-area and out-of-area opposition. The Alliance "overcome its old syndrome against so-called out of area operations" (Wörner, 1993g) says the SG. Because NATO goes out-of-area by using force without having any oppositions from the members inside. This means the step-by-step adoption of the "géométrie variable" (Wörner, 1993c) while considering which threats necessitate intervention or not, without geographical consideration. The NATO image as drawn in the SG speeches is an Alliance which started the change process and advances with no serious opposition.

In short, NATO's bureaucracy's leader position about the out-of-area norm change is positive: the SG welcomes the adaptation of the Alliance to meet new challenges. Wörner's pro-U.S. position and recognition of the American leadership show that he supports the U.S. executive power's initiative to change the old norm. Moreover, the SG describes Europe as unable to assure its own security and sees the security of West and East Europe as interrelated. It means that Wörner does not give so much flexibility to European countries on the subject of accepting or not the out-of-area norm change process: they have to follow the U.S. strategic leadership decisions. Yugoslavia in this situation was a very good case to test NATO out-of-area abilities and convince the undecided members of the norm change's indispensability.

In closing this section and given the results of the analysis, *I conclude that my expectation about the first step of the out-of-area norm's evolution is confirmed.* The U.S. executive power branch effectively initiated a norm change via its discourse during the Bosnian War case. It emphasized the "norm entrepreneur" role of the U.S. by constantly referring to its leadership role in the World and the Atlantic Alliance. Based on this fact, the president Clinton announced very clearly all the modalities of change required for the new out-of-area norm and wanted by the U.S. The persuasion of other members is done especially by using the idea of "failed states" in the new security context. Since the Bosnian War in ex-Yugoslavia was happening just in West European countries' next door, the point of it being in-area or out-of-area was not important. Military intervention of NATO in this case was justified according to the U.S. president in order to prevent the negative externalities spread out in neighbouring countries and the whole continent. The reaction of other members to this norm change initiative was rather mixed. In my study, the German chancellor accepted the start of the change process as it stands but was not so explicit about Germany's opinion regarding the future steps of a continued progress. He only explicitly noticed that his country is ready to cooperate if necessary. On the other side, as representing the opposing member, the Greek prime minister expressed a negative opinion with reference to the norm change. Nevertheless, Greece did not have the intention to block or prevent NATO's military operations in Bosnia. Finally, the SG of NATO welcomed the U.S. initiative to change and strongly advised the European countries to follow the American strategic leadership in this process. The **Table 3** summarizes the results for this section.

Table 3 Actors' characteristics in discourses for the Bosnian War case

Discursive subjects	Speakers			
	American president (Bill Clinton)	*German chancellor (Helmut Kohl)*	*Greek prime minister (Andreas Papandreou)*	*NATO's SG (Manfred Wörner)*
The actor itself	Active, cooperative, and leading member	Responsible and ready to contribute	Cooperative, hesitant on the Bosnian War	Active, cooperative, new roles, and buried the out-of-area problem
Yugoslavia	Problematic, needs help	Very tragic and set the limits	Risky, tragic	Opportunity, burden sharing
Europe	–	–	–	Weak and not capable of defending itself
NATO	Very active, unique, needs to change	Indispensable, active, and in transformation	Active and peaceful alliance	–
the U.S.	–	–	–	Powerful and the main security provider

5.3) The Iraq War case (2003–2011)

The Iraq War was another out-of-area issue in which NATO decided this time to not directly involve itself in the early steps of the conflict.[37] Such being the situation, I chose to include the Iraq War in my empirical analysis as a control case. In this way, I was able to look if an out-of-area issue in which NATO was not directly intervened had an impact or not on the evolution of the norm change process.

The conflict started with the invasion of Iraq in 2003 by the coalition of the willing led by the U.S. under the name "Operation Iraqi freedom". This out-of-area issue was very

---

[37] It is true that the NATO Training Mission-Iraq ('**NTM-I**') was established in 2004 and dismantled in 2011, existing as an out-of-area activity for the Alliance. However, it was only created after the collapse of the Ba'ath Party government and because of the Interim government's request in Iraq and the UNSC Resolution 1546. Moreover, it was not a combat mission but a training/mentoring one designed to assist the instruction of the indigenous security forces.

controversial and divided NATO members between themselves about what to do against the problem. On the one hand, the U.S. followed by major allied members as the U.K., Italy and Spain wanted the use of force to be considered in order to deal with the situation. On the other hand, members like France, Germany and Canada opposed this option and insisted on continued diplomatic means and weapons inspections. Despite the fact that NATO was not involved as an organization itself in the conflict, member allies naturally analysed and debated the situation also from the Atlantic Alliance perspective. Ergo, the case is convenient for a fruitful discourse analysis.

The U.K. is "tagged" as a leading member of the Iraq War case because after the U.S., it was the country who contributed the most – politically and militarily – to the conflict. The country was present at all early steps of the process which led to the war: UNSC resolution 1441, a draft resolution at the UN authorizing the use of force in Iraq, House of Commons approval for the invasion on 18 March 2003, and the participation of the British military in the first bombing campaign on March 20. Even though the "true" leader of the coalition of the willing is the U.S., I think the U.K. also played a very significant role in the campaign. I think in the Anglo-Saxon *duumviri* for this case, the U.K. was one of the main leaders even if not "the only one". I also decided to keep the U.K. for this case in order to not pick up the U.S. twice. The speaker for this country is Tony Blair: he was the prime minister of the U.K. from 1997 to 2007. The corpus contains extracts from 12 of his speeches held between 2002 and 2004 (Blair, 2002a, 2002b, 2002c, 2003a, 2003b, 2003c, 2003d, 2004; Bush, 2002, 2003a, 2003e, 2004). The dates correspond to one year before the start of the Iraq War and the expansion of combat violence to a peak with also an impeachment motion in preparation at the House of Commons against Blair. There are four discursive subjects for this case: the NATO cluster contains 15 equivalent classes, the U.K. eight, the coalition of the willing 13, and Europe nine.

The NATO subject in Blair's speeches is depicted as necessary, responsible and needing to change. The necessity of the Alliance is underlined through several adjectival and verbal predicates. It is an "important" military organization which provides protection for the member states' populations. More than only on the material side, it also protects "values" and constitutes a manifestation of the "international community's determination" (Bush, 2002). It "has its role today" which is "good and sound" (Bush, 2004). NATO is also a responsible alliance. Blair assigns a clear responsibility to NATO regarding the Iraq War case. For instance, about the post-conflict situation, he argues that the Alliance is fulfilling its mission in Iraq by training the Iraqi security forces through NTM-I. Therefore, it provides the expected support from the Atlantic Alliance to the transition process. Finally, NATO is also described as a military organization which needs to change. The alliance needs to adapt to the changing security context by being more "flexible and agile" (Blair, 2002c). Two important points are revealed about the expected change style that Blair wants. First, NATO should be "able to deploy rapidly" (Blair, 2002c) according to the prime minister: its timing is too slow. Second, more crucially, this deployment should be available for "wherever needed" (Blair, 2002c): the geographical constraints in connection with the out-of-area reluctance is no longer relevant for the 21st century. The NATO alliance in Blair's mind – and *de facto* the British government at that time – is an indispensable and forward-looking, active organization.

The U.K. discursive entity in the speeches is characterized as peaceful, helpful and seeking political solutions. The U.K. is a country which always favours peace over war and avoids involving itself in conflicts the most possible. Thus, Blair notes that the U.K. understands its people's angst about a pre-emptive military action in Iraq. By the same token, the U.K. is a country which prefers political solutions. Based on this commitment, the U.K. thinks that it is correct to "deal with Saddam through the United Nations" (Blair, 2002b). What's more, the country urges the need of a "political agenda" if the international community wants to continue on this road. Last but not least, the U.K. is a helpful country vis-à-vis Iraq. The interest of the State in Iraq is not limited to initial phases of the armed conflict but also the post-conflict reconstruction process. Besides its participation in the NTM-I, the U.K. is as well ready to help the Government of transition in its task of constructing a "democratic Iraq". The U.K. is then more than cooperative in general, according to Blair.

The coalition of the willing discursive subject is determined, successful and modest given Blair's speeches. The coalition is determined because it is ready to "do what's necessary" (Bush, 2002) to respond to the threat coming from the Iraqi government. It is the security guarantee of the Western Alliance and the only force who is capable of imposing UN resolutions. That's why they "started the war" (Blair, 2003a). The coalition is as well successful bearing in mind its past missions. The Western Alliance already effectively intervened in Bosnia, Kosovo, Afghanistan, and Sierra Leone to neutralize threats. As for the Iraq War, Blair states that the coalition does "have many allies" (Bush, 2003e) and receives support all around the world. Lastly, the coalition is a modest ad hoc alliance using a force proportional to the apparent threat. It acts in a "measured" and "calm" way, taking into consideration all alternative options. For instance, the coalition tried to reach a political agreement at the UN framework before initiating a military intervention. It is interesting to see that Blair tries to establish a natural link between the ad hoc coalition of the willing intervening in the Iraq War and the NATO framework by referring to past military missions in which the Atlantic alliance was directly involved. It implicitly supposes that the main source of power in all these missions is the same whether officially under the NATO banner or not.

The "Europe" group is designated as potentially ready to act but disunited. It takes every UNSC's resolutions very seriously and is ready to do whatever necessary if there is no concrete progress in the disarmament process of Iraq. But, at the same time, Europe also acknowledges the necessity to have a common voice against a "common threat" (Blair, 2003c). In facts, there are important disagreements between Western countries about the legacy and the justification of the military intervention in Iraq. Therefore, the military intervention option also has many opponents inside.

To review, the U.K. follows the norm entrepreneur concerning the out-of-area norm change process: NATO effectively needs to change. The Atlantic Alliance is an indispensable organization for the security of the member countries and needs to adapt itself to the changing world because there is no alternative to replace it. The U.K. in these turbulent times is described as a cooperative and helpful country. It is probably to point out its role in the continued persuasion of other members about the usefulness and the harmless nature of the norm's new version. Interestingly, the speaker creates a relationship between the potential success of the coalition of the willing and past NATO missions. It has as effect to blur the difference between the ad hoc coalition regrouped for the Iraq War and the NATO framework. The result is more legitimacy in the discourse for the coalition and the creation of an idea in minds about a common source of power from which the coalition and NATO live on. In this situation, Europe has the potential to contribute to Iraq War but is disunited. A common voice and strategic thinking against threats are needed as claimed by Blair which implicitly means the acceptance of the new out-of-area norm by all member allies. Otherwise, it won't be effective.

I chose Spain as the "contributing member" for the Iraq War case owing to its political and military support to the coalition during the conflict. Although the military contribution of the country is not so great, its political support is incontestable: Spain was one of the three countries – together with the U.S. and the U.K. – who jointly prepared a draft resolution on Iraq at the UN in order to set a deadline for compliance. If the draught had been put for a formal vote and passed, it would have been legitimate to use force after the deadline in order to disarm the Iraqi government. Spain was also the country who acted as an interlocutor between the coalition and the European Union ('**EU**') while trying to convince some other EU member countries of the benefits of an intervention. The speaker I kept for this country is José María Aznar: he was the prime minister of Spain from 1996 to 2004. The speech corpus in his case consists of paragraphs extracted from five speeches held between 2001 and 2003 (Aznar, 2003; Bush, 2001, 2003b, 2003c, 2003d). The dates correspond to several months before the September 11 attacks while under the Islamic terrorism threat and several weeks after the invasion of Iraq. Again, four discursive subjects emerge from the results. The NATO cluster includes ten predicates, Spain 14, the coalition of the willing 14, and the Europe nine.

The NATO subject in the speeches is represented as an essential, changing, and expanding alliance. The Alliance is the key actor for the "transatlantic security" (Bush, 2001) and permits sustained relations between the U.S. and the EU through defensive trade and military socialization. NATO is as well a military organization in constant change in order to meet the requests arising from the new century's security challenges. It is adapting itself by "strengthen its capabilities" to "meet new missions and challenges" (Bush, 2001). Interestingly, in the speeches, Aznar abolishes the distinction between in and out-of-area by stating that NATO should serve "an undivided Europe and Euro-Atlantic area" (Bush, 2001). By the same logic, the Alliance is also expanding by accepting new members from the former USSR countries. It also creates relationships with non-member countries (e.g., Russia) through new frameworks such as the PfP. The NATO in Aznar's speeches is not an alliance that should be confined in a status quo.

Spain as illustrated by Aznar is a responsible, active, and contributing country. It is a state conscious of its roles and tasks vis-à-vis the International community with reference to the Iraq War. As other members of the coalition, Spain participates in this intervention because it thinks there is no alternative options to secure the Euro-Atlantic area. Nevertheless, it is also ready to support other initiatives in order to establish "the International legality" (Aznar, 2003) and put an end to the armed conflict. It is in any case committed to post-conflict Iraq reconstruction and faces all the risks immediately, while also complying "to the International community" (Aznar, 2003). Spain is an active country doing a lot in the conflict. It assumes its role in the "fighting against terrorism and WMDs" (Aznar, 2003) and facing other threats. In the Iraq War case, Spain stands firm and do whatever necessary as a NATO and EU member of the coalition. Finally, Spain is also a country who contributes in general to the Western Alliance security and Iraq. At the international level, it pursues a policy of "strengthen the Transatlantic link" (Bush, 2003c) and is ready to "co-sponsor" another UNSC resolution about the Iraq War. Specifically regarding to Iraq War, Spain proportionally contributes to the coalition in order to face the threat posed by Saddam. So, the Spain of Aznar is a cooperative and pro-U.S. member of NATO.

The coalition of the willing, as it stands in the speeches, is reported as cooperative, responsible, and active. Once again, the coalition is an entity which uses the UN platform actively and prepare resolutions in order to have a political solution first. It tried to "achieve the greatest possible agreement" (Bush, 2003d) to have more legitimacy for its actions. The coalition is a responsible group too. It is committed to face any threat after having tried other non-military options and being sure that there is no satisfying alternative. In Iraq, the coalition has always done what is needed. Lastly, it is also very active since it contributed to the liberation of Iraq and the building of a new democratic society. The predicates about the coalition of the willing are more of a defensive nature against the opponents than only qualifying. It was the case in Blair's speeches as well.

Europe in Aznar's discourses is a geographical entity which is united and contributing to the Atlantic Alliance. Europe is an "essential" part of the NATO. It is "fully coordinated" (Bush, 2001) in itself and also vis-à-vis the alliance. The Europe as described by Aznar contributes to the Atlantic Alliance and accomplishes its duty whenever necessary. It develops its capacities and commits resources to the Alliance. Moreover, Europe is also capable of intervening to resolve problems by itself when NATO cannot be used. In this latter case, European countries who are not EU members are incorporated either.

To conclude, Spain accepts the out-of-area norm change process initiated by the U.S.: NATO needs to change constantly in order to be updated. In comparison with the German chancellor's speeches, the executive leader of the contributing country in this case is more direct and explicit about its opinion. Aznar says clearly that NATO should protect the extended Euro-Atlantic area without in or out considerations. Furthermore, the expansion of the Alliance is also welcomed. The speaker categorizes his country as very cooperative and ready to follow the majority in any change process in NATO. As plus, Europe is no longer portrayed as an entity which is in constant disagreement and unable to assure its own defence. Contrary to the predicates in the Bosnian case, the "Europe" discursive subject is now an entity which is united and assuming its part of the burden sharing. It could even resolve its problems alone when NATO cannot intervene. So, Spain as a "newly" democratic country and late member of the Alliance accepts the norm change without hesitation in order to gain more legitimacy in the Western Alliance.

Canada for the Iraq War is taken as the "opposing member" due to its formal position to not to participate in the invasion of Iraq in 2003. Even if Canada did participate in the First Gulf War in 1991 and the Kosovo war – this one under NATO and without UN resolution –, it refused to take part in the Iraq War because of the absence of a UNSC resolution to use force. Even though some facts[38] show that the real position of Canada in regard to the Iraq War is more controversial than it appears (e.g., participation of a hundred Canadian exchange officers to the U.S. in the early phases of the invasion, alleged documents on a clandestine support proposal made to the U.S. by high-ranking Canadian bureaucrats, Jean Chrétien's moral support to the coalition and assistance to NATO in other areas, etc.), I think we can still assume that the

---

[38] For more detailed information about these facts, please see Stein and Lang (2007).

country is an opposing member to the operation compared to direct participants in the conflict. The speaker I chose for this country is Jean Chrétien: he was the 20th prime minister of Canada from 1993 to 2003. The corpus data for him is composed of extracts from five of his speeches held between February to November 2003 (Chrétien, 2003a, 2003b, 2003c, 2003d, 2003e). All these texts are in their original French version and analysed accordingly. The time frame corresponds to one month before the invasion of Iraq and several weeks after the big increase of the insurgency in the conflict region. There are three main clusters in Chrétien's speeches. The NATO discursive subject contains three equivalent classes, Canada 30, and finally the U.S. only one.

The NATO subject in the prime minister's speeches is invoked as an essential and multilateral organization. It is an indispensable and active actor for the security of the Western Alliance. At the same time, it only extends its mandate with UNSC resolutions given its cooperative and multilateral nature. Interestingly, the U.S. in Chrétien's speeches is portrayed as a friend and ally, even the "best" one. It is without any doubt the manifestation of the prime minister's moral support to the coalition.

The Canada discursive subject in the speeches is characterized as a cooperative, active, and multilateral entity. It is a cooperative country because even without participating in the Iraq War, it tries to contribute one way or another to the resolution of security problems threatening the Western Alliance. It recognized the importance of American determination in the problem and "salué le leadership de le [sic] Président Bush" (Chrétien, 2003a). Moreover, it did support initial UNSC's resolutions in the past about Iraq's aggressive behaviour which also contained in themselves serious retaliation in case of non-compliance. Canada is a "friend" of the U.S. and the U.K. and prays for the success of the coalition even if it does not participate. It is ready to contribute to the "reconstruction of Iraq" and the continuing "fight against terrorism" (Chrétien, 2003b) alongside with its historical and natural allies. Secondly, Canada is an active entity as well, even though it does not take part in the Iraq War. It did participate in several NATO's military expeditions in the past (e.g., Bosnia, Kosovo). It is deploying a significant number of troops in different NATO missions (e.g., the Gulf) and will "replace the expeditionary troops" (Chrétien, 2003d) in Afghanistan. Finally, Canada attaches a big importance to the multilateralism in the World, especially in security affairs. It refused to participate in the Iraq War because there was no international legacy to conduct such a mission. For Canada from this point, a UNSC resolution is a "condition à toute participation à une campagne militaire" (Chrétien, 2003c). Having this in mind, it is interesting to see how Chrétien justifies Canada's participation in the Kosovo war under NATO banners, whereas there was no UNSC resolution authorizing the use of force either. He says that Canada gone there to "stop the genocide" (Chrétien, 2003d), which is to implicitly say that under these kinds of circumstances having a UNSC resolution or not is not binding. The "Canada" subject emerging from these predicates is an independent country adopting its own way and having a solid argument against the change of the norm in the Atlantic Alliance.

To put it succinctly, Canada has rather a negative opinion about the out-of-area norm change initiated by the U.S. initiative: there are legal limits to what can be done or not outside of the treaty area. Before everything else, NATO is an international organization which should respect multilateralism. Canada is not completely against the norm change but put a condition in order this new version to be legitimate: a UNSC resolution is necessary for every out-of-area intervention. The only exception that can be made to this prerequisite is the breach of a peremptory norm such as genocide by an aggressor. As we can see here, the opinion of the opposing member to the norm change in this step of cascade is different from the emergence one. Canada does not reject completely the idea of change but specifies it by adding a legalistic argument.[39] It also has a more explicit and clear position compared to the Greek one. Canada

---

[39] For further details about the content of this argument and NATO's subordination to the international law, please have a look at Simma (1999).

respects the U.S. leadership and the purpose of the coalition but underlines the importance of multilateralism when initiating an important change.

The 10th SG of NATO from 1999 to 2004 is George Robertson. During the initial phases of the conflict and until the end of his mandate, he tried to manage intra-alliance differences as good as he could. The corpus for him is constructed with extracts from 24 of his speeches held from March 2002 to December 2003 (Robertson, 2002a, 2002b, 2002c, 2002d, 2002e, 2002f, 2002g, 2003a, 2003b, 2003c, 2003d, 2003e, 2003f, 2003g, 2003h, 2003i, 2003j, 2003k, 2003l, 2003m, 2003n, 2003o, 2003p, 2003q). The timeline corresponds to one year before the start of the war and two days after the capture of Saddam Hussein. There are three main discursive subjects in the discourses. NATO cluster is composed of 75 predicates, the coalition of the willing three, and Iraq seven.

The coalition of the willing in Robertson's speeches is an active and united subject. It is the entity that "alerts people" (Robertson, 2002f) of the Iraqi regime's dangerous behaviour and prepares military options. The coalition is united around a common goal too. These results are quite the same across countries and cases.

The "Iraq" cluster as depicted in the speeches is in need and in relation with international organizations. According to Robertson, the conflict in the region should be concluded as soon as possible and humanitarian "aid should be delivered" (Robertson, 2003h). *De facto*, casualties also need to be diminished. It is also a subject of interest for prominent international organizations such as the UN and NATO. Iraq "lies with the UN" (Robertson, 2002d) and Robertson remarks that the Atlantic Alliance might interfere much more within the conflict whatever the way. Even without a formal participation in the early steps of the war, the SG signals the possibility of NATO's contribution to the conflict in any manner.

The NATO subject in the extracts is ready, active, cooperative, and in a transformation entity. The Alliance is ready to face most of the new threats of this century. It is, on the one hand, ready to do more in missions already in place such as in Afghanistan. On the other hand, the SG says that NATO could do more in future regarding the Iraq War. New future missions are not excluded. NATO is already an active organization as well, whether directly or indirectly linked to the Iraq War. It makes decisions very rapidly and needed only "24 hours to get a top statement on Iraq" (Robertson, 2002c). NATO already gone "out-of-continent" (Robertson, 2003g) by combatting terrorists in Afghanistan. Even if not formally involved in Iraq, NATO supports "Poland and Spain for their role in the stabilization of post-Saddam Iraq" (Robertson, 2003k). The Atlantic Alliance is a cooperative organization. Against the new threats, it works with the U.S. to overcome them and constructs a consensus inside NATO. The nineteen-member countries still do make decisions in consensus. The Alliance supports all the UN initiatives concerning Iraq, whether the resolutions or compliance to them. The multilateralism is an important commitment of NATO. Finally, and most importantly, NATO as portrayed by Robertson is still in a transformation phase. The relevant capabilities of the organization need some further adaptation to deal with new threats. Characters of new threats are more or less agreed on but there is still debates inside the Alliance on how to face them. In general terms, Robertson assures that there is no more a powerful disagreement inside NATO over whether the Alliance "could or should go "out-of-area"" (Robertson, 2003q). This debate was "old and artificial" (Robertson, 2003m) and makes no sense in the new century: the Alliance must be ready to intervene wherever and whenever needed for the Western Alliance security. This does not mean to play a "global policeman" (Robertson, 2003f) role but, at the same time, does also not mean to limit NATO's effectiveness in superficial boundaries. The Alliance is gradually "turning the rhetoric of transformation into reality" (Robertson, 2003e). Nonetheless, there are still cases on which the allies disagree such as the Iraq one. But these disagreements concern only the means to deal with the issue and not the core of the problem or the fact of going out-of-area, as stated by Robertson. The NATO of the SG is an alliance which changed a lot but is still in transformation.

To sum up, the out-of-area norm change is now well underway, and the SG of NATO is clearly in favour of it. The SG completely adopts the change's necessity rhetoric advanced by the norm entrepreneur and the main followers. In fact, the Alliance already changed to some extent and is dealing with some of the new threats as in the case of Afghanistan. However, the process is not over, and further transformation is needed. Especially given that in some cases disagreements still appear on the means of dealing with problems (e.g., Iraq War).

In summarizing this section's findings, *I conclude that my expectation about the cascade step of the norm's change is also confirmed.* The U.K. executive power branch conformed to the out-of-area norm change and contributed to the progress of the process through formal persuasion. It underlined the indispensability of the Alliance and the necessity to change for overcoming new threats. The link created between the potential success of the coalition of the willing and past NATO missions in Blair's discourse is another side of the persuasion about the superficiality of the out-of-area debates. Without the adoption of the new norm in NATO by all members – given the consensual decision-making structure – , it won't be effective. Spain as a contributing country in this case also accepts the change, even more explicitly than Germany in the Bosnian War. As a "latecomer" in the alliance, it is as well in favour of the expansion. We can more easily see the effects of the change process while looking at the Canadian's position. It is an "opposing member" but does not completely reject the out-of-area norm's change idea: it only points out the importance of multilateralism and adds a legalistic condition about UNSC resolutions and peremptory norms. Lastly, the SG of NATO recognizes that the Alliance already changed, and he is happy about the consequences of the adaptation. Nevertheless, he advises the continuation of the transformation because there are still members who reject the new version of the norm on some points, which causes occasional disagreements. The table **below** shows the main results for this section.

Table 4 Actors' characteristics in discourses for the Iraq War case

Discursive subjects	Speakers			
	British prime minister (Tony Blair)	*Spanish prime minister (José Maria Aznar)*	*Canadian prime minister (Jean Chrétien)*	*NATO's SG (George Robertson)*
The actor itself	Peaceful, helpful, and seeking political solutions	Responsible, active, and contributing	Cooperative, active, and multilateral	Ready, active, cooperative, and in transformation
Iraq	–	–	–	In need and relation with international organizations
Europe	Ready to act but disunited	United and contributing	–	–
NATO	Necessary, responsible, and in need to change	Essential, changing, and expanding	Essential and multilateral	–
the Coalition of the willing	Determined, successful, and modest	Cooperative, responsible, and active	–	Active and united
the U.S.	–	–	Best friend and ally	–

5.4) The Libyan War case (2011)

The NATO-led military intervention in Libya was the last time – for the moment – that the Alliance directly and offensively involved itself in an out-of-area issue. The conflict started with the Arab Spring protests in 2011 during which protesters and security forces clashed in Benghazi. With the spread of protests all over the country, a civil war started opposing Muammar Gaddafi's regime and rebels organized around the National Transitional Council ('**NTC**'). After Gaddafi's sustained non-compliance with UN calls to end the violence, the UNSC resolution 1973 authorized the creation of a no-fly zone which NATO ensured through a bombing campaign from March. Subsequent to several months of fight, the war ended with the capture and kill of Colonel Gaddafi in 20–23 October. As a result, NATO terminated its operation by the end of the month too. This military intervention created some controversies inside the Atlantic Alliance between members. Criticisms were concentrated around the Responsibility to Protect ('**R2P**') concept, civilian losses, legacy of the out-of-area involvement, presence of foreign troops on the ground, and the classical burden sharing issue (Bachman, 2017; Haesebrouck, 2017; Song, 2016). It opposed Germany, Poland, Spain, Turkey, Netherlands on the one camp and the U.S., the U.K., France and others on the opposite. Some bilateral and informal meetings happened inside NATO before the start and at earlier steps of the campaign, in order to convince a few key members in critical junctures (Davidson, 2013; Theiss, 2015).

France is labelled as the "leading member" in the Libyan War because it was the first country who recognized the political legitimacy of the NTC and also the first one who started air strikes against the regime's forces. At the end, it was also the country who realized most of the strikes in general. Even if, technically speaking, the war has cost less to France compared to the U.K. and the U.S., France clearly had the political leadership in this conflict. The speaker for this case is Nicolas Sarkozy: he was the President of France from 2007 to 2012. The corpus data for him embraces extracts from eight of his speeches held from February 2011 to August 2011 (Sarkozy, 2011a, 2011b, 2011c, 2011d, 2011e, 2011f, 2011g, 2011h). All of his speeches are kept in their original French version and analysed accordingly. The dates correspond to one month before the start of the military intervention and several days after the fall of Tripoli. There are four main discursive subjects emerging from the results. The NATO cluster comprises 11 equivalent classes, France 25, Europe four, and the coalition of the willing five.

The coalition of the willing in Sarkozy's speeches is described as diversified and coordinated. It has the "contrôle politique" (Sarkozy, 2011d) of the operation and conducts strikes under the hospices of NATO. The coalition is also diversified and does not contain only Atlantic Alliance members. The "Europe" subject is portrayed as united and concerned. There are no disagreements on Libya according to Sarkozy and European countries are concerned of the situation in Libya because it is their neighbour. The Libyan military intervention underlines an interesting feature of the new out-of-area missions: the ad hoc coalitions and NATO framework are now mixed and can work together, as in practices and minds of most of the allies.

The NATO cluster in the extracts is reported as a functional and helpful organization. It is described once again as an "outil indispensable" (Sarkozy, 2011e) which does accomplish its tasks as it should be, without any problems. Furthermore, it was more than helpful during the Libyan War according to Sarkozy, especially in terms of coordination. In fact, NATO was the platform for military coordination of the coalition and decided the targets and timelines of strikes. With this technical support, the Alliance "served" very well the coalition of the willing led by the Europeans and its political objectives. Sarkozy does not even mention the fact of NATO going out-of-area, which shows that the French executive power branch at that time completely internalized the new version of the norm.

The "France" subject in the speeches is a responsible, cooperative, and active entity vis-à-vis the Libyan conflict. It is responsible because it does take into account different sensibilities of countries and is careful about a military intervention in Libya. It follows the events closely and considers the victims, condemns the violence. It rather prefers a political solution than a military one, whether under the NATO banner or not. France is also – as most of the other countries – a cooperative player which is in a constant contact with its partners and international organizations regarding the issue. It works closely with the U.K. for putting up a plan. It is also monitoring potential "décisions que pourrait prendre le Conseil de sécurité" (Sarkozy, 2011a). It recognizes the importance of working with the UN and non-Western partners in order for the coalition to have more legitimacy. Finally, it is an active subject. France started to work on a plan from the earlier steps of the conflict. When the situation became worse, it also discussed possible operation scenarios with other actors. Sarkozy once again does not make any substantial difference between a NATO-led or an ad hoc coalition-led military operation.

In fine, France seems to have completely internalized the new version of the out-of-area norm at that time. On the one hand, Sarkozy does not even mention the concept either as a point of debate or only as a fact. It shows France executive power branch's indifference towards the old version of the norm. On the other hand, Sarkozy welcomes the cooperation of the ad hoc coalition of the willing with NATO and their share of the political and military control. More than the out-of-area issue, the participation of non-members and non-Western partners in a military operation supervised by NATO does also not cause any problem to France.

Turkey is the "contributing country" for the Libyan War case due to its modest contribution to the Western Alliance from the end of March. The country was supportive of the Libyan opposition but dissatisfied with the violence and clearly against a foreign military intervention at the earlier steps of the conflict. It even prevented for some time the passing of the operation's military coordination to NATO because of its reluctance over an offensive intervention. After several bilateral meetings with the U.S. officials (Davidson, 2013), it finally accepted the issue and decided to participate in the NATO-led mission. It contributed up to a total sum of 300 million dollars to the Libyan War. I think despite its initial hesitations, we can still label Turkey as a "contributing country" to the NATO mission. The speaker for this country is Recep Tayyip Erdoğan: he was the 25th Prime Minister of Turkey from 2003 to 2014. The data to be analysed for him consists of extracts from six of his speeches held between November 2010 and April 2011 (Erdoğan, 2010, 2011a, 2011b, 2011c, 2011d, 2011e). Four of these six speeches were translated from Turkish into English by myself for the analysis (Erdoğan, 2010, 2011a, 2011b, 2011c). The dates correspond to four months before the start of the conflict and several weeks after the Turkish participation in the NATO-led operation. There are two main discursive subjects in the results which are NATO and Turkey. The NATO cluster is composed of 15 equivalent classes and Turkey 21.

The NATO subject in the speaker's speeches is characterized as a defensive alliance which should intervene in Libya only very cautiously. The speaker refers to the core feature of NATO which is the defence of its members and their territorial integrity. Its offensive quality is only hypothetical in a case of an attack from outside. Therefore, in NATO's mind and documents "no country should be targeted as a threat source" (Erdoğan, 2010) concludes the prime minister. The potential NATO interference in Libya is looked as impossible at first. The prime minister thought that an intervention there makes nonsense and would be useless with "dangerous consequences" (Erdoğan, 2011a). Moreover, since the Libyan War is an out-of-area issue, NATO could intervene only if a direct attack occurs from there to the treaty area says the speaker. Otherwise, it is "unthinkable" (Erdoğan, 2011c). However, once the operation started, speeches are revised and three conditions are added for a NATO operation in Libya: protecting the civilians, not considering the distribution of natural resources and helping the Libyan people to take back the control of their country in their hands. Even if controversial, the vision of Turkey about NATO and its relation to out-of-area issues is very different in this case compared to other contributing countries in the past.

The "Turkey" cluster is helpful, cooperative, and demanding in the results. From the beginning of the conflict, it entered in conversation with both parties and provided advice to the regime about how to handle the protests. It putted in place an "intense diplomatic traffic" (Erdoğan, 2011b). After the implication of NATO, it also helped "the implementation of the arms embargo as well as the provision of humanitarian aid" (Erdoğan, 2011d). Turkey cooperated with the actors inside Libya and the U.K. in order to end the conflict. From its participation to the NATO-led operation, it cooperated with member allies too. Finally, Turkey is a demanding country regarding the military intervention in Libya. While against it at first, the country accepted it only under some conditions. It wishes to see the conflict concludes as soon as possible and casualties to be terminated. Turkey wants the military intervention led by NATO "to be conducted efficiently" (Erdoğan, 2011d). The country's position as described by the speaker is very attentive and sceptical at the same time towards the NATO mission.

To synopsize, Turkey does not seem to have internalized the new version of the out-of-area norm at that time. Contrary to other actors in the Libyan case and the previous Iraqi one, it brings again the old version of the norm – which should be forgotten by now – in the debate. This idea constituted for the country an important source of motivation to be against a NATO-led military intervention in Libya. Although Turkey reconsidered its opinion and decided to participate in the military operations afterwards, it was only conditional to some requirements and the contribution was rather modest and symbolic.

The Czech Republic is chosen as the "opposing member" to the Libyan War because of its none participation in the enforcement of the UNSC resolution by NATO. The country in reality was very divided over a potential military intervention in Libya and several contradictory statements were made by the foreign and prime ministers before the start of the conflict. However, with the start of the no-fly zone enforcement and air strikes, they decided to not to participate in the mission. They even adopted a pro-Gaddafi position in the earlier steps of the conflict because of concerns over the stability in the region. The speaker I kept for this country is Václav Klaus: he was the 2nd President of the Czech Republic from 2003 to 2013. The text corpus for him contains extracts from three of his speeches held between June 2010 to September 2011 (Klaus, 2010, 2011a, 2011b). The dates correspond to one year before the start of the conflict and one month before the conclusion of the NATO operation. There are three main clusters apparent in the results. The NATO subject consists of seven predicates, the Czech Republic five and the solution five as well.

The solution subject in Klaus's speeches is described as needing to be indigenous and detailed. For the citizens to be in comfort with the solution offered, the speaker argues that it should be originated from the country itself. Furthermore, the plan of the solution should also need to be detailed and realistic for it to be easily applicable on the conflictual situation. The Czech Republic of Klaus is also against foreign interventions as in the Turkish case.

The NATO cluster in the extracts is portrayed as an entity which should be active vis-à-vis Libya without intervening militarily. Klaus recognizes that NATO defence policy "starts far beyond its borders" (Klaus, 2010) and therefore what is happening in Libya may be of a natural concern for the organization. Nevertheless, the Atlantic Alliance must rely on other means than the military ones (e.g., diplomatic and political efforts) in order to deal with the case. Klaus has a negative opinion about too much interference in domestic affairs of foreign States which can result in bad consequences for everyone in the region. The President then acknowledges the impact of out-of-area issues on NATO even without the presence of a direct attack.

The "Czech Republic" subject is cautious and realistic, according to predicates in the extracts. It urges the Western Alliance to take steps more slowly regarding the Libyan War. Concretely, it expresses its concerns about the support to the NTC and the establishment of a no-fly zone. The Czech Republic is realistic as well and knows that the problems in the region cannot be resolved immediately. Klaus cites the transformation of its own country as an example for the ones in trouble. Nonetheless, he underlines at the same time the absence of required "preconditions" for a successful transformation in countries experiencing the Arab Spring. Klaus is more in favour of independent solutions than foreign-prepared formulas.

To conclude, the Czech Republic seems to have partially internalized the new version of the out-of-area norm in NATO at that time. It accepts the impact that an out-of-area issue might have on the treaty area whether a direct attack towards the Alliance occurs or not. But on the other hand, it disagrees on the means to deal with the problems. The country as represented by

Klaus adopts a strong non-interventionist principle towards external countries and prefers the use of diplomatic tools to resolve the problems.

Finally, the 12th SG of NATO from 2009 to 2014 is Anders Fogh Rasmussen. He was very concerned and reactive towards the Libyan War from the earlier steps of the conflict. The data to analyse for him corresponds to extracts from 17 of his speeches held between March and September 2011 (Rasmussen, 2011a, 2011b, 2011c, 2011d, 2011e, 2011f, 2011g, 2011h, 2011i, 2011j, 2011k, 2011l, 2011m, 2011n, 2011o). Some of the extracts are conserved in their original French version and analysed accordingly. The dates correspond to the start and one month before the end of the military intervention in Libya. Two main discursive subjects emerge from the results. The NATO cluster is composed of 78 equivalent classes and the Operation 16.

The NATO subject is described as proactive, cooperative, fast, responsible, and defensive. The Alliance adopted a proactive stance towards the Libyan War from the very beginning, according to the SG. NATO prepared itself militarily and politically to any potential threat that may come from the Libyan conflict to its area. It was ready to assume its role if anything had gone wrong. It is also an organization which acts very fast. Rasmussen says that NATO consensually made the decision to take control of the operation in "6 days" (Rasmussen, 2011c). He also recognizes the lack of the necessary material contributions during the operation despite the fast and flexible decision. The Atlantic Alliance is a cooperative entity too. It decided to participate in the operations in order to enforce the UNSC resolution and was in "constant contact with regional and international partners" (Rasmussen, 2011d). It also assumed to have relations within the rebel groups to Gaddafi. NATO is as always portrayed as a responsible military organization. The Alliance gone in the region only in order to enforce the resolution – no more – and protect the civilians. It aims to contribute to the conclusion of the conflict as soon as possible, without having a political agenda for afterwards. It is determined to continue the intervention until there is a clear evidence that a peaceful outcome will be reached soon.

Finally, and most importantly, the SG states clearly the core purpose of the Alliance which is the defence of its members. In the earlier phases of the Libyan civil war, he said that NATO has no "intention to intervene" (Rasmussen, 2011b, 2011k) on several occasions. He underlined the defensive nature of the Alliance: the main purpose of NATO is to defend the treaty area against external attacks. Beyond this classical "territorial defence" task, NATO has no "plans to intervene in new areas" (Rasmussen, 2011o) apart the Libyan War case. It is interesting to see how the SG of NATO is using arguments from the beginning of the post-Cold War context to justify the position of the Alliance.

The operation cluster in the speeches is presented as successful with a strong legal basis. Given the main legal source of the NATO-led operation which is the UNSC resolution, there is no obstacle in using force in the Libyan War according to the international law. The operation was also a very good example of NATO providing a swift response to a crisis and using its capabilities efficiently. The insistence of the SG on the legal basis is an important part of the argumentation about NATO's implication in the coalition of the willing.

To summarize, the internalization process of the new out-of-area norm also seems to not to have finished on the NATO bureaucracy side at that time. The SG resorts to classical arguments dating from the Cold War such as the core defensive function of NATO and its right to react only in a case of attack. It also shows NATO's unwillingness to implicate itself in the Libyan War at the earlier phases of the conflict and insistence of not having any plans to intervene in other areas afterwards. Even if, controversially, he praised the merits of the NATO-led military operation in Libya and said that it could become a "model", it was only after being sure of strict conditions that NATO accepted to take control of the no-fly zone and arms embargo: legal basis, regional support and incontestable necessity.

In closing this sub-chapter, *I assume without hesitation that my last expectation about the norm's change is falsified.* Despite 20 years of ongoing change process, the new version of the norm is still not completely internalized in the organization. In this Libyan War case, the French position was positive and there was no questioning at all of the norm's evolution. However, the Turkish executive power branch position was negative. Besides its change of opinion about NATO contribution to the operation – due to bilateral pressions from the U.S. —, the Turkish prime minister mentioned in his speeches the old difference between in-area and out-of-area while underlining its legitimacy. Therefore, the fact of even mentioning this rule as a well-founded one is a sufficient evidence of non-internalization, at least discursively. The Czech Republic as an opposing member seems to have partially internalized the new norm but only at the ideational level: it still disagrees on the SOPs to adopt towards these issues. This shows a kind of non-compliance as well. Finally, and most crucially, NATO's bureaucracy also seems to be still in track regarding the internalization of the norm. The SG of the Alliance talking about the core defensive purpose and a right to react only in a case of attack constitute a blatant evidence of the non-internalization. The new version of the norm is not taken for granted and even if NATO accepted to lead the military operation in Libya, every future decision will depend on the circumstances and strict prerequisites, urges the SG. The table **below** presents the technical findings in this section.

Table 5 Actors' characteristics in discourses for the Libyan War case

Discursive subjects	Speakers			
	French President (Nicolas Sarkozy)	*Turkish Prime Minister (Recep Tayyip Erdoğan)*	*Czech President (Václav Klaus)*	*NATO's SG (Anders Fogh Rasmussen)*
The actor itself	Responsible, cooperative, and active	Helpful, cooperative, and demanding	Cautious and realistic	Proactive, cooperative, fast, responsible, and defensive
Europe	United and concerned	–	–	–
NATO	Functional and helpful	Defensive, should intervene cautiously	Should be active without military intervention	–
the Coalition of the willing	Diversified and Coordinated	–	–	–
the Operation	–	–	–	Successful with a strong legal basis
The Solution	–	–	Needs to be indigenous and detailed	–

5.5) Final remarks and thoughts

The discourse on the out-of-area norm in NATO changed step by step in 20 years without being successful to completely internalize the new version of it in the organization. In the first step of emergence, the U.S. executive power branch as a norm entrepreneur successfully pushed for the new version of the out-of-area norm among the fellow member countries and the NATO bureaucracy in general. Having relied mostly on the failed states' argument, it rather had positive reactions from other allied countries and especially the NATO SG. In the second step of cascade, the U.K. executive power branch started to contribute to the change process through formal persuasion by blurring the difference between ad hoc coalitions and NATO, while referring to the Atlantic Alliance's indispensability. It also had mainly positive returns from the members and support from the SG to continue the change process. In the supposed final step of internalization, I should have had all the actors inside the organization to have completely internalized the new version of the out-of-area norm in their discourses and minds. Besides the positive French example, it was not the case for the two other countries that I looked for: they still had the old distinction in their discourse. Moreover, the new version of the norm was not taken for granted by the SG of NATO as well. The **Table 6** below presents the general results of this dissertation.

Table 6 The general findings of the dissertation

Expectations	Actors			
	Leading member	*Contributing member*	*Opposing member*	*NATO's bureaucracy*
Confirmed: U.S. executive => norm entrepreneur => new version of the out-of-area norm	Failed states argument (U.S.)	Necessity of change argument (Germany)	Peaceful alliance argument (Greece)	New threats and U.S. leadership argument
Confirmed: U.K. executive => norm follower => massive ratification	Common voice argument (U.K.)	Regular updates argument (Spain)	Legal limits argument (Canada)	Further transformation needed
Falsified: SOPs change => complete internalization	Taken for granted (France)	*"Old" in-area vs. out-of-area argument* (Turkey)	*Non-interventionism argument* (the Czech Republic)	*Defensive function & Reactive nature argument*

I think there are at least two potential explanations for the unexpected result in the last step of internalization. First, because of changing political contexts, important national differences, and consensual decision-making, the reaction of NATO towards out-of-area issues cannot be analysed under the "norm" concept/idea. Therefore, it would mean that there were not SOPs to deal with out-of-area problems during the Cold War in the first place. Every issue is analysed on a case-by-case basis by the allied members and reacted accordingly, without having a pre-defined general framework in minds. Second, one can also argue that there is a fundamental difference between the old and new versions of the out-of-area norm in NATO: the former is a primary and the latter is a secondary norm. The old version of the norm has a strong legal basis designed by the Article 6 of the NATO treaty: we can assume that it is a kind of "Constitutional norm". On the contrary, the new version of the norm being promoted is defined by other complementary documents such as strategic concepts, doctrines, discourses, etc.: it is rather a secondary norm. Consequently, the old version of the norm is not flexible in interpretation and every member of the Alliance should comply with it at first. The interpretation of the new version is more flexible, and countries could choose to comply or not depending on the case. A complete internalization of the new version of the norm could occur only if the NATO treaty is reviewed accordingly, which is politically impossible for the moment.

Conclusion

In this dissertation, I investigated the discursive change of the out-of-area norm in NATO from 1980 to 2011. For the late-Cold War period, I relied on several historical documents and conducted an archival analysis in order to show the status of the norm during this period. Early American initiatives to change it are revealed as well. For the post-Cold War period, I used predicate analysis to analyse the discourses of selected member countries executive leaders and the SG's about the norm. It is done through three empirical cases: the Bosnian War, the Iraq War and the Libyan War. I based my general expectation concerning this period on the norm change theoretical argument of Finnemore and Sikkink (1998).

I found for the late-Cold War period that the American initiatives and backstage lobbying to start a change process of the out-of-area norm were not successful. Despite internal differences in the U.S. between departments, the executive power wanted a change. However, the European members of the Alliance were sceptical about a potential transformation because of the Cold War context and the presence of the Soviet Union who could retaliate. By the same token, NATO's bureaucracy was also against a mandate extension due to its potential divisive nature on the members. Regarding the post-Cold War period, I found that the change process of the old norm was started and advanced to some extent, without being successful to completely internalize the new version of the norm for all members. Notwithstanding 20 years, there are still member countries – and even the SG – referring to the old distinction between in and out-of-area while confronted to a problematic situation.

The main contribution of this study is the additional clarification on the changing attitude of NATO vis-à-vis out-of-area issues since the end of the Cold War. Through extensive empirical data and rigorous method, I was able to show the importance of intra-alliance dynamics on the change of the norm. Each different steps of the initial political agreement – or disagreements – on this subject are disclosed with their impact on the evolution of the process. Furthermore, I demonstrate that changing an old norm which has a legal basis is very difficult and can only be done through the change of the legal text itself.

There are also some limitations in this work that I recognize and will mention without regret. First, one could legitimately ask if we can talk about a norm when it is not completely internalized. Either for the old or the new version of the "supposed" norm, these results maybe suggest that it does not exist and the attitude of NATO towards out-of-area issues is not guided by a general framework. Second, even if we assume that the norm exists, my way of observing it might be seen as problematic. Because I take for granted that the norm is carried by member states – and the NATO bureaucracy – and manifested through their executive leaders, I do not pay consideration to change of individuals and governments. Since we cannot always assume that different people and governments will hold on to the same norm, there might be a bias in my reasoning about the evolution process. Third and by the same logic, given that I focus only on the executive power branch for the purpose of comparability, there may be another bias about the source of information. As seen for the Cold War period, different departments inside a same country could have distinct visions on out-of-area issues. Therefore, the results could have been different if I had focused on other departments too.

In terms of future research, it might be interesting to have a look at concrete practices done or not during each out-of-area crisis, through interviews or technical manuals of different operations.[40] It is important because what is "said" on the paper and "done" on the terrain are most of the time different. A comparison between the discourse and the practice could be done then while observing the similarities, differences, and the evolution of these trends. Unfortunately, because of technical, budgetary, and access constraints, I was not able to work with these data. I leave these challenges to future searchers.

---

[40] Instead of analysing discourses.

Data Availability

The data and other relevant materials related to this dissertation can be found at https://drive.google.com/open?id=1AExkK5MpPkLrqkpOzKChRIAAJQbx-7KI, an online file hosting and synchronization service owned by Google.

References

Aznar, J. M. (2003). Aznar statement on Iraq war. Madrid: AP Archive. Retrieved from http://www.aparchive.com/metadata/youtube/db7a929826d6bc3e3a0ef48e402e89a9

Bachman, J. (2017). Libya: A UN Resolution and NATO's Failure to Protect. In *Land of Blue Helmets* (1 ed., pp. 212-230). Oakland: University of California Press.

Behnke, A. (2013). *NATO's security discourse after the Cold War: representing the West*. London: Routledge.

Bennett, D. S. (1997). Testing Alternative Models of Alliance Duration, 1816-1984. *American Journal of Political Science*, 41(3), 846-878. doi:10.2307/2111677

Bent, F. (2006). Five Misunderstandings About Case-Study Research. *Qualitative Inquiry*, 12(2), 219-245. doi:10.1177/1077800405284363

Blair, T. (2002a, April 7). [Speech at the George Bush Senior Presidential Library]. Retrieved from http://www.britishpoliticalspeech.org/speech-archive.htm?speech=281

Blair, T. (2002b, September 10). [Speech to TUC Conference]. Retrieved from http://www.ukpol.co.uk/tony-blair-2002-speech-to-tuc-conference/

Blair, T. (2002c). Statement by The Prime Minister of the United Kingdom, The Rt Hon. Tony Blair [Press release]. Retrieved from https://www.nato.int/cps/su/natohq/opinions_19650.htm?selectedLocale=en

Blair, T. (2003a, September 30). [Leader's speech]. Retrieved from http://www.britishpoliticalspeech.org/speech-archive.htm?speech=184

Blair, T. (2003b, February 15). [Speech at Labour's local government, women's and youth conferences]. Retrieved from http://www.britishpoliticalspeech.org/speech-archive.htm?speech=306

Blair, T. (2003c, July 17). [Speech to the US Congress]. Retrieved from http://www.britishpoliticalspeech.org/speech-archive.htm?speech=285

Blair, T. (2003d, March 18). [Statement on Iraq in the House of Commons]. Retrieved from http://www.ukpol.co.uk/tony-blair-2003-statement-on-iraq/

Blair, T. (2004, March 5). ["Prime Minister warns of continuing global terror threat", Sedgefield]. Retrieved from http://www.britishpoliticalspeech.org/speech-archive.htm?speech=282

Blumenau, B., Hanhimäki, J. M., & Zanchetta, B. (Eds.). (2018). *New Perspectives on the End of the Cold War: Unexpected Transformations?* (1 ed.). London: Routledge.

Bowman, R. C. (1981). *BILATERAL MEETING WITH THE TURKS -- 15 MAY 1981, 0930-- CONFERENCE ROOM #7, NATO HEADQUARTERS*. (CIA-RDP84B00049R001403560034-1). USA: CIA Retrieved from https://www.cia.gov/library/readingroom/docs/CIA-RDP84B00049R001403560034-1.pdf

Branch, T. (2009). *The Clinton tapes : wrestling history with the President*. London: Simon and Schuster.

Bremer, P. L. (1982a). *INTERAGENCY REVIEW GROUP MEETING ON NSSD 1-82 US NATIONAL SECURITY STRATEGY*. (CIA-RDP85M00366R000100060015-0). USA:

CIA   Retrieved   from   https://www.cia.gov/library/readingroom/docs/CIA-RDP85M00366R000100060015-0.pdf

Bremer, P. L. (1982b). *NATO SUMMIT PREPARATIONS*. (CIA-RDP84B00049R000500980004-1).   USA: CIA   Retrieved   from https://www.cia.gov/library/readingroom/docs/CIA-RDP84B00049R000500980004-1.pdf

Budge, L. D. (1987). *ALLIED COMMISSION ON OUT-OF-AREA ISSUES ACT, H.R. 2805*. (CIA-RDP90M00004R001000090003-5).   USA: CIA   Retrieved   from https://www.cia.gov/library/readingroom/docs/CIA-RDP90M00004R001000090003-5.pdf

Bush, G. W. (2001). Joint Statement by President George W. Bush and President José Maria Aznar. Retrieved June 13, 2018, from The American Presidency Project http://www.presidency.ucsb.edu/ws/?pid=45959

Bush, G. W. (2002). Remarks Prior to Discussions with Prime Minister Tony Blair of the United Kingdom and an Exchange With Reporters in Prague, Czech Republic. Retrieved June 13, 2018, from The American President Project http://www.presidency.ucsb.edu/ws/?pid=7

Bush, G. W. (2003a). Declaration on Iraq by President George W. Bush and Prime Minister Tony Blair. Retrieved June 13, 2018, from The American Presidency Project http://www.presidency.ucsb.edu/ws/?pid=62950

Bush, G. W. (2003b). The President's News Conference with President Jose Maria Aznar of Spain. Retrieved June 13, 2018, from The American Presidency Project http://www.presidency.ucsb.edu/ws/?pid=63566

Bush, G. W. (2003c). The President's News Conference With President Jose Maria Aznar of Spain in Crawford, Texas. Retrieved June 13, 2018, from The American Presidency Project http://www.presidency.ucsb.edu/ws/?pid=138

Bush, G. W. (2003d). The President's News Conference with Prime Minister Jose Manuel Durao Barroso of Portugal, President Jose Maria Aznar of Spain, and Prime Minister Tony Blair of the United Kingdom in the Azores, Portugal. Retrieved June 13, 2018, from The American Presidency Project http://www.presidency.ucsb.edu/ws/?pid=62764

Bush, G. W. (2003e). The President's News Conference with Prime Minister Tony Blair of the United Kingdom at Camp David, Maryland. Retrieved June 13, 2018, from The American Presidency Project http://www.presidency.ucsb.edu/ws/?pid=64773

Bush, G. W. (2004). The President's News Conference with Prime Minister Tony Blair of the United Kingdom in Istanbul. Retrieved June 13, 2018, from The American Presidency Project http://www.presidency.ucsb.edu/ws/?pid=72676

Choi, S.-W., & James, P. (2014). Why Does the United States Intervene Abroad? Democracy, Human Rights Violations, and Terrorism. *Journal of Conflict Resolution*, 60(5), 899-926. doi:10.1177/0022002714560350

Chrétien, J. (2003a, February 13). [Discours du Premier ministre canadien, Jean Chrétien, devant le Chicago Council on Foreign Relations]. Retrieved from http://www.voltairenet.org/article9061.html

Chrétien, J. (2003b, April 8). [Déclaration de Jean Chrétien]. Retrieved from http://www.voltairenet.org/article9489.html

Chrétien, J. (2003c, March 17). [Déclaration sur l'Irak de Jean Chrétien, Premier ministre du Canada]. Retrieved from http://www.voltairenet.org/article9365.html

Chrétien, J. (2003d, March 9) *Entretien de Jean Chrétien, Premier ministre du Canada, avec la chaîne ABC/Interviewer: G. Stephanopoulos*. This Week, ABC, Washington D.C. Retrieved from http://www.voltairenet.org/article9366.html

Chrétien, J. (2003e, November 13). [Notes pour un discours du Premier ministre Jean Chrétien à l'occasion de la soirée hommage au Premier ministre]. Retrieved from https://www.canada.ca/fr/nouvelles/archive/2003/11/notes-discours-premier-ministre-jean-chretien-occasion-soiree-hommage-premier-ministre.html

Chun, K. H. (2013). NATO: Adaptation and Relevance for the 21st Century. *Journal of International and Area Studies*, 20(2), 67-82.

CIA. (1986). *WESTERN EUROPE-UNITED STATES: DIFFERENCES OVER POLICY TOWARD LIBYA HIGHLIGHT DEEPER SPLITS WITHIN THE ALLIANCE*. (CIA-RDP86T01017R000404120001-9). Washington D.C.: CIA Retrieved from https://www.cia.gov/library/readingroom/docs/CIA-RDP86T01017R000404120001-9.pdf

Clinton, W. J. (1993). The President's News Conference With Chancellor Helmut Kohl of Germany. Retrieved March 26, from The American Presidency Project http://www.presidency.ucsb.edu/ws/?pid=46377

Clinton, W. J. (1994a). Remarks and an Exchange With Reporters on Bosnia. Retrieved June 13, 2018, from The American Presidency Project http://www.presidency.ucsb.edu/ws/?pid=49354

Clinton, W. J. (1994b). Remarks Announcing the NATO Decision on Air Strikes in Bosnia and an Exchange With Reporters. Retrieved June 13, 2018, from The American Presidency Project http://www.presidency.ucsb.edu/ws/?pid=49509

Clinton, W. J. (1994c). Remarks at the Bosnian Federation Agreement Signing Ceremony. Retrieved June 13, 2018, from The American Presidency Project http://www.presidency.ucsb.edu/ws/?pid=49829

Clinton, W. J. (1994d). Remarks to the North Atlantic Council in Brussels. Retrieved June 13, 2018, from The American Presidency Project http://www.presidency.ucsb.edu/ws/?pid=49710

Clinton, W. J. (1994e). The President's News Conference With Chancellor Helmut Kohl of Germany in Bonn. Retrieved June 13, 2018, from The American Presidency Project http://www.presidency.ucsb.edu/ws/?pid=50471

Clinton, W. J. (1994f). The President's News Conference With European Union Leaders in Brussels. Retrieved June 13, 2018, from The American Presidency Project http://www.presidency.ucsb.edu/ws/?pid=49765

Clinton, W. J. (1994g). The President's News Conference With Prime Minister Andreas Papandreou of Greece. Retrieved June 13, 2018, from The American Presidency Project http://www.presidency.ucsb.edu/ws/?pid=50023

Clinton, W. J. (1995a, November 27). [Address on Bosnia]. Retrieved from https://millercenter.org/the-presidency/presidential-speeches/november-27-1995-address-bosnia

Clinton, W. J. (1995b). Remarks Following Discussions With Chancellor Helmut Kohl of Germany and an Exchange With Reporters in Baumholder. Retrieved June 13, 2018, from The American Presidency Project http://www.presidency.ucsb.edu/ws/?pid=50844

Clinton, W. J. (1995c). The President's News Conference With Chancellor Helmut Kohl of Germany. Retrieved June 13, 2018, from The American Presidency Project http://www.presidency.ucsb.edu/ws/?pid=50959

Clinton, W. J. (1996a, October 22). [Remarks to people of Detroit]. Retrieved from https://www.nato.int/cps/su/natohq/opinions_25141.htm?selectedLocale=en

Clinton, W. J. (1996b). The President's News Conference With Chancellor Helmut Kohl of Germany in Milwaukee. Retrieved June 13, 2018, from The American Presidency Project http://www.presidency.ucsb.edu/ws/?pid=52859

Croft, S., Howorth, J., Terriff, T., & Webber, M. (2000). NATO's Triple Challenge. *International Affairs (Royal Institute of International Affairs 1944-)*, 76(3), 495-518.

Davidson, J. W. (2013). France, Britain and the intervention in Libya: an integrated analysis. *Cambridge Review of International Affairs*, 26(2), 310-329. doi:10.1080/09557571.2013.784573

Derleth, J. (2015). Enhancing interoperability: the foundation for effective NATO operations. *NATO Review*(2), 182-190.

Doyle, M. W. (1983). Kant, Liberal Legacies, and Foreign Affairs. *Philosophy & Public Affairs*, 12(3), 205-235.

Duffield, J. S. (1994). NATO's Functions after the Cold War. *Political Science Quarterly*, 109(5), 763-787. doi:10.2307/2152531

Erdoğan, R. T. (2010, November 23). [Recep Tayyip Erdoğan's party group speech at the Grand National Assembly of Turkey]. Retrieved from https://tr.wikisource.org/wiki/Recep_Tayyip_Erdoğan%27ın_23_Kasım_2010_tarihli_TBMM_grup_konuşması

Erdoğan, R. T. (2011a). Erdoğan: Libya'ya NATO müdahalesi faydasız. *Bloomberg HT*. http://www.bloomberght.com/haberler/haber/867164-erdogan-libyaya-nato-mudahalesi-faydasiz

Erdoğan, R. T. (2011b). Erdoğan: Operasyon işgale dönüşmemeli. *Cumhuriyet*. http://www.cumhuriyet.com.tr/haber/diger/231692/Erdogan__Operasyon_isgale_donu_smemeli.html

Erdoğan, R. T. (2011c). NATO'nun ne işi var Libya'da? *Sabah*. https://www.sabah.com.tr/gundem/2011/02/28/natonun_ne_isi_var_libyada

Erdoğan, R. T. (2011d). Speech Delivered by H.E. Prime Minister Recep Tayyip Erdoğan on Libya [Press release]. Retrieved from http://www.mfa.gov.tr/speech-delievered-by-h_e_-prime-minister-recep-tayyip-erdogan-on-libya-_ankara_-7-april-2011_.en.mfa

Erdoğan, R. T. (2011e). Turkish Prime Minister press conference [Press release]. Retrieved from https://www.gov.uk/government/speeches/turkish-prime-minister-press-conference

Finnemore, M., & Sikkink, K. (1998). International Norm Dynamics and Political Change. *International Organization*, 52(4), 887-917.

Haesebrouck, T. (2017). NATO Burden Sharing in Libya: A Fuzzy Set Qualitative Comparative Analysis. *Journal of Conflict Resolution*, 61(10), 2235-2261. doi:10.1177/0022002715626248

Hanhimäki, J. M., Schoenborn, B., & Zanchetta, B. (2012). *Transatlantic relations since 1945: an introduction*. London: Routledge.

Harris, Z. S. (1952). Discourse Analysis. *Language*, 28(1), 1-30. doi:10.2307/409987

Hendrickson, R. C. (2006). *Diplomacy and war at NATO : the secretary general and military action after the Cold War*. Columbia: University of Missouri Press.

Hendrickson, R. C. (2010). NATO's Secretaries-General: ORGANIZATIONAL LEADERSHIP IN SHAPING ALLIANCE STRATEGY. In *NATO in Search of a Vision* (pp. 51-74). Washington D.C.: Georgetown University Press.

Hofmann, S. C. (2013). *European security in NATO's shadow : party ideologies and institution building*. Cambridge, England ; New York: Cambridge University Press.

Hofmann, S. C. (2017). Party preferences and institutional transformation: revisiting France's relationship with NATO (and the common wisdom on Gaullism). *Journal of Strategic Studies*, 40(4), 505-531. doi:10.1080/01402390.2016.1227258

Hofmann, S. C., & Mérand, F. (2012). Regional organization *à la carte*: the effects of institutional elasticity. In T. V. Paul (Ed.), *International relations theory and regional transformation* (pp. 133-157). New York: Cambridge University Press.

Hofmann, S. C., & Yeo, A. I. (2015). Business as usual: The role of norms in alliance management. *European Journal of International Relations*, 21(2), 377-401. doi:10.1177/1354066114533978

ICTY. (2017). The Conflicts. *Mechanism for International Criminal Tribunals*. Retrieved from http://www.icty.org/en/about/what-former-yugoslavia/conflicts

Ikenberry, G. J. (2001). *After victory : institutions, strategic restraint, and the rebuilding of order after major wars*. Princeton New Jersey: Princeton University Press.

Kempf, O. (2010). *L'OTAN au XXIe siècle: la transformation d'un héritage*. Perpignan: Artege.

Kitchen, V. M. (2010a). NATO's out-of-area norm from Suez to Afghanistan. *Journal of Transatlantic Studies*, 8(2), 105-117. doi:10.1080/14794011003760269

Kitchen, V. M. (2010b). *The globalization of NATO: intervention, security and identity*. New York: Routledge.

Klaus, V. (2010, June 30). [Notes for the Independence Day Speech]. Retrieved from https://www.klaus.cz/clanky/2634

Klaus, V. (2011a, March 11). [Notes for the European Council on Libya]. Retrieved from https://www.klaus.cz/clanky/2790

Klaus, V. (2011b, September 23). [Speech of the President at the General Debate of the 66th Session of the UN General Assembly]. Retrieved from https://www.klaus.cz/clanky/2932

Kohl, H. (1992, April 3). [Zielvorstellungen und Chancen für die Zukunft Europas]. Retrieved from http://helmut-kohl.kas.de/index.php?menu_sel=17&menu_sel2=126&menu_sel3=&menu_sel4=&msg=1446

Kohl, H. (1994, January 19). [Rede bei einem internationalen Symposium anlässlich des 175-jährigen Bestehens der Rheinischen Friedrich-Wilhelms-Universität Bonn]. Retrieved from http://www.helmut-kohl.de/index.php?menu_sel=17&menu_sel2=&menu_sel3=&menu_sel4=&msg=1472

Kohl, H. (1996a, June 4). [Ansprache vor dem Nordatlantischen Kooperationsrat in Berlin]. Retrieved from http://helmut-kohl.kas.de/index.php?menu_sel=17&menu_sel2=126&menu_sel3=&menu_sel4=&msg=1638

Kohl, H. (1996b, February 3). [Rede bei der 33. Münchner Konferenz für Sicherheitspolitik in München]. Retrieved from http://helmut-kohl.kas.de/index.php?menu_sel=17&menu_sel2=126&menu_sel3=&menu_sel4=&msg=1608

Kratochwil, F. V. (1989). *Rules, norms, and decisions on the conditions of practical and legal reasoning in international relations and domestic affairs*. Cambridge: Cambridge University Press.

Lasater, J. R. (1982). *Memorandum of Conversation*. (233). Washington D.C.: Government Printing Office Retrieved from https://history.state.gov/historicaldocuments/frus1981-88v13/d233

Lepgold, J. (1998). NATO's Post-Cold War Collective Action Problem. *International Security*, 23(1), 78-106. doi:10.2307/2539264

Liebig, M. (1990). NATO: "Out of area" or out of business? *Executive Intelligence Review*, 17(50), 33-35.

Liland, F. (1999). *Keeping NATO out of trouble: NATO's non-policy on out-of-area issues during the Cold War* (Vol. 4). Oslo: Institutt for Forsvarsstudier.

Lundestad, G. (2003). *The United States and Western Europe since 1945 : from "Empire" by Invitation to Transatlantic Drift*. Oxford etc.: Oxford University Press.

Mahoney, J. (2015). Process Tracing and Historical Explanation. *Security Studies*, 24(2), 200-218. doi:10.1080/09636412.2015.1036610

Manning, C., Surdeanu, M., Bauer, J., Finkel, J., J. Bethard, S., & McClosky, D. (2014, June 23-24). *The Stanford CoreNLP Natural Language Processing Toolkit*. Paper presented at the Proceedings of 52nd Annual Meeting of the Association for Computational Linguistics: System Demonstrations, Baltimore, Maryland USA.

March, J. G., & Olsen, J. P. (2013). The Logic of Appropriateness. In R. E. Goodin (Ed.), *The Oxford Handbook of Political Science* (pp. 479-497). New York: Oxford University Press.

McCalla, R. B. (1996). NATO's persistence after the cold war. *International Organization*, 50(3), 445-475. doi:10.1017/S0020818300033440

Michas, T. (2002). *Unholy alliance : Greece and Milošević's Serbia*. College Station: Texas A & M Univ. Pr.

Mihalache, O.-C. (2017). NATO's 'Out of Area' Operations: A Two-Track Approach. The Normative Side of a Military Alliance. *Croatian International Relations Review*, 23(80), 233-258. doi:10.1515/cirr-2017-0027

Milliken, J. (1999). The Study of Discourse in International Relations: A Critique of Research and Methods. *European Journal of International Relations*, 5(2), 225-254. doi:10.1177/1354066199005002003

Moore, R. R. (2007). *NATO's new mission: projecting stability in a post-Cold War world*. Westport: Praeger Security International.

NATO. (1982). DOCUMENT ON INTEGRATED NATO DEFENCE BONN [Press release]. Retrieved from http://archives.nato.int/uploads/r/null/1/4/140136/PRESS_COMMUNIQUE_M3_82_18_ENG.pdf

NIC. (1986). *THE EUROPEAN ALLIES' VIEW OF THE THIRD WORLD AND THE REAGAN DOCTRINE*. (CIA-RDP87R00529R000100060004-4). USA: CIA Retrieved from https://www.cia.gov/library/readingroom/docs/CIA-RDP87R00529R000100060004-4.pdf

Olson, M. (1971). Increasing the Incentives for International Cooperation. *International Organization*, 25(4), 866-874.

Parenti, F. M., & Adda, I. (2017). Are we going to live in a post-NATO world? A critical perspective on trends, obstacles and possibilities. *GeoJournal*, 82(2), 345-354. doi:10.1007/s10708-015-9693-8

Rasmussen, A. F. (2011a, March 30). ["Hungry for Security: Can NATO help in a humanitarian crisis?"]. Retrieved from https://www.nato.int/cps/su/natohq/opinions_71864.htm?selectedLocale=en

Rasmussen, A. F. (2011b). Joint press point with NATO Secretary General Anders Fogh Rasmussen and the Prime Minister of Montenegro Mr. Igor Lukšić [Press release]. Retrieved from https://www.nato.int/cps/su/natohq/opinions_71145.htm?selectedLocale=en

Rasmussen, A. F. (2011c). Monthly press briefing by NATO Secretary General [Press release]. Retrieved from https://www.nato.int/cps/su/natohq/opinions_77640.htm?selectedLocale=en

Rasmussen, A. F. (2011d). Monthly press conference by NATO Secretary General [Press release]. Retrieved from https://www.nato.int/cps/su/natohq/opinions_75067.htm?selectedLocale=en

Rasmussen, A. F. (2011e). NATO After Libya: The Atlantic Alliance in Austere Times. *Foreign Affairs*, 90(4), 2-6.

Rasmussen, A. F. (2011f). NATO Secretary General's monthly press conference [Press release]. Retrieved from https://www.nato.int/cps/su/natohq/opinions_72205.htm?selectedLocale=en

Rasmussen, A. F. (2011g). NATO Secretary General's statement on Libya no-fly zone [Press release]. Retrieved from https://www.nato.int/cps/su/natohq/news_71763.htm?selectedLocale=en

Rasmussen, A. F. (2011h, May 30). [NATO: preparing for the unpredictable]. Retrieved from https://www.nato.int/cps/su/natohq/opinions_74854.htm?selectedLocale=en

Rasmussen, A. F. (2011i, May 9). [NATO: Preserving Unity Through Solidarity]. Retrieved from https://www.nato.int/cps/su/natohq/opinions_73606.htm?selectedLocale=en

Rasmussen, A. F. (2011j, March 10). [Opening remarks by NATO Secretary General Anders Fogh Rasmussen at the meeting of NATO Defence Ministers]. Retrieved from https://www.nato.int/cps/su/natohq/opinions_71398.htm?selectedLocale=en

Rasmussen, A. F. (2011k). Press Briefing by NATO Secretary General Anders Fogh Rasmussen preceding the March NATO Defence Ministerial Meeting [Press release]. Retrieved from https://www.nato.int/cps/su/natohq/opinions_71257.htm?selectedLocale=en

Rasmussen, A. F. (2011l). Press conference by NATO Secretary General Anders Fogh Rasmussen after the working lunch of NATO Ministers of Foreign Affairs with Libya partners [Press release]. Retrieved from https://www.nato.int/cps/su/natohq/opinions_72443.htm?selectedLocale=en

Rasmussen, A. F. (2011m, April 15). [Questions and answers at the press conference by NATO Secretary General Anders Fogh Rasmussen on the second day of the meeting of NATO Foreign Affairs Ministers]. Retrieved from https://www.nato.int/cps/su/natohq/opinions_72785.htm?selectedLocale=en

Rasmussen, A. F. (2011n, March 17). ["Strengthening European security" Speech by NATO Secretary General Anders Fogh Rasmussen]. Retrieved from https://www.nato.int/cps/su/natohq/opinions_71564.htm?selectedLocale=en

Rasmussen, A. F. (2011o, September 30). [Towards NATO's Chicago Summit]. Retrieved from https://www.nato.int/cps/su/natohq/opinions_78600.htm?selectedLocale=en

Ringsmose, J. (2010). NATO Burden-Sharing Redux: Continuity and Change after the Cold War. *Contemporary Security Policy, 31*(2), 319-338. doi:10.1080/13523260.2010.491391

Risse-Kappen, T. (1996). Collective Identity in a Democratic Community: The Case of NATO. In P. J. Katzenstein (Ed.), *The culture of national security: norms and identity in world politics* (Vol. New directions in world politics, pp. 357-399). New York: Columbia University Press.

Robertson, G. (2002a, March 7). ["NATO And The Challenge Of Terrorism: Reflections On The Way Forward" Speech by NATO Secretary General Lord Robertson at The Dutch Group Of Liberal International]. Retrieved from https://www.nato.int/cps/su/natohq/opinions_19859.htm?selectedLocale=en

Robertson, G. (2002b, April 10). ["NATO on the road to Prague" Speech by NATO Secretary General, Lord Robertson at the Council on Foreign Relations]. Retrieved from https://www.nato.int/cps/su/natohq/opinions_19850.htm?selectedLocale=en

Robertson, G. (2002c, November 21). [Press conference by Lord Robertson, NATO Secretary General following the Meeting of the North Atlantic Council at the level of Heads of State and Government]. Retrieved from https://www.nato.int/cps/su/natohq/opinions_19664.htm?selectedLocale=en

Robertson, G. (2002d, November 11). [Press Point by NATO Secretary General, Lord Robertson and Vladimir Putin, President of the Russian Federation at the Hilton Hotel].

Retrieved from https://www.nato.int/cps/su/natohq/opinions_19614.htm?selectedLocale=en

Robertson, G. (2002e, December 9). [Questions and Answers with NATO Secretary General, Lord Robertson at the ITAR-TASS press agency]. Retrieved from https://www.nato.int/cps/su/natohq/opinions_19604.htm?selectedLocale=en

Robertson, G. (2002f, June 6). [Statement to the press by NATO Secretary General, Lord Robertson at the press conference following the meeting of the North Atlantic Council at the level of NATO Ministers of Defence]. Retrieved from https://www.nato.int/cps/su/natohq/opinions_19773.htm?selectedLocale=en

Robertson, G. (2002g, November 8). ["The Future of a Larger NATO" Speech by NATO Secretary General, Lord Robertson at the EPC Breakfast Policy Briefing]. Retrieved from https://www.nato.int/cps/su/natohq/opinions_19615.htm?selectedLocale=en

Robertson, G. (2003a, February 20). [Building a Transatlantic Consensus NATO Secretary General Lord Robertson's Remarks at the European Institute Washington, D.C.]. Retrieved from https://www.nato.int/cps/su/natohq/opinions_20377.htm?selectedLocale=en

Robertson, G. (2003b, October 1). [Change and continuity by Lord Robertson]. Retrieved from https://www.nato.int/cps/su/natohq/opinions_20537.htm?selectedLocale=en

Robertson, G. (2003c, November 25). [Closing remarks by NATO Secretary General, Lord Robertson at the 2nd European Parliament meetings on Defence]. Retrieved from https://www.nato.int/cps/su/natohq/opinions_20516.htm?selectedLocale=en

Robertson, G. (2003d, December 15). [Comments by NATO Secretary General, Lord Robertson on the Policy Recommendations adopted by the NATO Parliamentary Assembly at its Forty Ninth Annual Session in Orlando]. Retrieved from https://www.nato.int/cps/su/natohq/opinions_20356.htm?selectedLocale=en

Robertson, G. (2003e, October 13). [NATO's Transformation Remarks by NATO Secretary General, Lord Robertson at the Geneva Centre for Security Policy]. Retrieved from https://www.nato.int/cps/su/natohq/opinions_20567.htm?selectedLocale=en

Robertson, G. (2003f). Press conference by NATO Secretary General, Lord Robertson following the meeting of the North Atlantic Council at the level of Ministers of Foreign Affairs [Press release]. Retrieved from https://www.nato.int/cps/su/natohq/opinions_20443.htm?selectedLocale=en

Robertson, G. (2003g). Press conference by NATO Secretary General, Lord Robertson following the working session for Allied and Invitee Defence Ministers [Press release]. Retrieved from https://www.nato.int/cps/su/natohq/opinions_20546.htm?selectedLocale=en

Robertson, G. (2003h). Press statement by NATO Secretary General, Lord Robertson and George Papandreou, Minister of Foreign Affairs of Greece, EU following the NATO-EU informal working luncheon at NATO Headquarters [Press release]. Retrieved from https://www.nato.int/cps/su/natohq/opinions_20503.htm?selectedLocale=en

Robertson, G. (2003i). Press Statement by NATO Secretary General, Lord Robertson following the meeting of the North Atlantic Council at the level of Foreign Ministers [Press release]. Retrieved from https://www.nato.int/cps/su/natohq/opinions_20504.htm?selectedLocale=en

Robertson, G. (2003j, January 24). [Speech by NATO Secretary General, Lord Robertson]. Retrieved from https://www.nato.int/cps/su/natohq/opinions_20409.htm?selectedLocale=en

Robertson, G. (2003k, November 6). [Speech by NATO Secretary General, Lord Robertson at the OSCE Permanent Council in Vienna, Austria]. Retrieved from https://www.nato.int/cps/su/natohq/opinions_20525.htm?selectedLocale=en

Robertson, G. (2003l, November 24). [Speech by NATO Secretary General, Lord Robertson at the Winston Churchill Lecture]. Retrieved from https://www.nato.int/cps/su/natohq/opinions_20517.htm?selectedLocale=en

Robertson, G. (2003m, February 17). [Speech by NATO Secretary General, Lord Robertson to the Bulgarian Parliament]. Retrieved from https://www.nato.int/cps/su/natohq/opinions_20390.htm?selectedLocale=en

Robertson, G. (2003n, May 26). [Speech by NATO Secretary General, Lord Robertson to the NATO Parliamentary Assembly, Prague]. Retrieved from https://www.nato.int/cps/su/natohq/opinions_20472.htm?selectedLocale=en

Robertson, G. (2003o). Statement to the Press by Lord Robertson, NATO Secretary General following NAC Foreign Ministers meeting [Press release]. Retrieved from https://www.nato.int/cps/su/natohq/opinions_20362.htm?selectedLocale=en

Robertson, G. (2003p, February 8). [Toward A New Transatlantic Consensus Speech by NATO Secretary General, Lord Robertson at the Munich Conference on Security Policy]. Retrieved from https://www.nato.int/cps/su/natohq/opinions_20378.htm?selectedLocale=en

Robertson, G. (2003q, January 1). [Transforming NATO]. Retrieved from https://www.nato.int/cps/su/natohq/opinions_20403.htm?selectedLocale=en

Rynning, S. (2005). *NATO renewed: the power and purpose of transatlantic cooperation*. New York: Palgrave Macmillan.

Sarkozy, N. (2011a, March 2). [Conférence de presse conjointe de MM. Nicolas Sarkozy, Président de la République, et Jacob Zuma, Président de la République d'Afrique du Sud, sur les relations franco-sud-africaines et sur la situation politique en Libye et en Côte d'Ivoire]. Retrieved from http://discours.vie-publique.fr/notices/117000562.html

Sarkozy, N. (2011b, March 24). [Conférence de presse de M. Nicolas Sarkozy, Président de la République, notamment sur l'Union européenne et l'intervention militaire en Libye sous mandat de l'ONU]. Retrieved from http://discours.vie-publique.fr/notices/117000748.html

Sarkozy, N. (2011c, March 11). [Conférence de presse de M. Nicolas Sarkozy, Président de la République, notamment sur la position de l'Union européenne face à la situation politique et humanitaire en Libye]. Retrieved from http://discours.vie-publique.fr/notices/117000613.html

Sarkozy, N. (2011d, March 25). [Conférence de presse de M. Nicolas Sarkozy, Président de la République, notamment sur le pacte pour l'Euro, la sécurité nucléaire et sur l'intervention militaire en Libye]. Retrieved from http://discours.vie-publique.fr/notices/117000749.html

Sarkozy, N. (2011e, August 31). [Déclaration de M. Nicolas Sarkozy, Président de la République, notamment sur le développement de l'Afrique, la démocratisation dans les pays arabes, l'avenir de l'Union européenne et la crise économique et financière]. Retrieved from http://discours.vie-publique.fr/notices/117001884.html

Sarkozy, N. (2011f, May 4) *Extraits d'un entretien de M. Nicolas Sarkozy, Président de la République, dans "L'Express", sur la lutte contre le terrorisme, la situation dans les pays arabes, l'avenir du processus de paix israélo-palestinien, la construction européenne et l'immigration et sur le bilan de sa politique depuis son élection en 2007.* L'Express, Vie Publique, Paris. Retrieved from http://discours.vie-publique.fr/notices/117001086.html

Sarkozy, N. (2011g, March 10). [Lettre de MM. Nicolas Sarkozy, Président de la République, et David Cameron, Premier ministre du Royaume-Uni de Grande-Bretagne et d'Irlande du Nord, adressée à M. Herman Van Rompuy, Président du Conseil européen, sur les mesures préconisées par la France et le Royaume Uni pour mettre fin aux violences en Libye]. Retrieved from http://discours.vie-publique.fr/notices/117000611.html

Sarkozy, N. (2011h, February 25). [Point de presse conjoint de MM. Nicolas Sarkozy, Président de la République, et Abdullah Gül, Président de la République de Turquie, sur les relations franco-turques, la situation politique dans les pays arabes et sur la position de la France face à l'adhésion éventuelle de la Turquie à l'Union européenne]. Retrieved from http://discours.vie-publique.fr/notices/117000532.html

Simma, B. (1999). NATO, the UN and the Use of Force: Legal Aspects. *European Journal of International Law*, 10, 1-22.

Sloan, S. R. (2010). *Permanent alliance ? : NATO and the transatlantic bargain from Truman to Obama*. New York: Continuum.

Song, Y. (2016). The US commitment to NATO in the post-Cold War period – a case study on Libya. *Journal of Transatlantic Studies*, 14(1), 83-113. doi:10.1080/14794012.2015.1125165

Stein, J. G., & Lang, J. E. (2007). *The unexpected war : Canada in Kandahar*. Toronto: Viking Canada.

Stratfor (2014). Current and Past NATO missions. Retrieved from https://worldview.stratfor.com/article/natos-post-cold-war-missions

Stuart, D. T., & Tow, W. T. (1990). *The limits of alliance ; NATO out-of-area problems since 1949*. Baltimore ; London: The Johns Hopkins University Press.

Søndergaard, R. S. (2015). Bill Clinton's 'Democratic Enlargement' and the Securitisation of Democracy Promotion. *Diplomacy & Statecraft*, 26(3), 534-551. doi:10.1080/09592296.2015.1067529

Terriff, T. (2003). The CJTF Concept and the Limits of European Autonomy. In J. Howorth & J. T. S. Keeler (Eds.), *Defending Europe: The EU, NATO, and the Quest for European Autonomy* (pp. 39-59). New York: Palgrave Macmillan US.

Theiss, J. (2015). NATO: The Process of Negotiating Military Intervention in Libya. In I. W. Zartman (Ed.), *Arab Spring: Negotiating in the Shadow of the Intifadat* (pp. 332-363). Athens: University of Georgia Press.

Vergilius, P. M. (Ed.) (2002 [-29 and -19]). *Enéide / T. 1, Livres I-IV* (3e tirage de l'éd. revue et corrigée / par R. Lesueur ed.). Paris: Les Belles Lettres.

Wallander, C. A. (2000). Institutional Assets and Adaptability: NATO after the Cold War. *International Organization*, 54(4), 705-735.

Wallander, C. A., & Keohane, R. O. (1999). Risk, threat and security institutions. In H. Haftendorn, R. O. Keohane, & C. A. Wallander (Eds.), *Imperfect Unions: Security Institutions over Time and Space* (pp. 21-47). Oxford: Oxford University Press.

Walt, S. M. (1997). Why alliances endure or collapse. *Survival*, 39(1), 156-179. doi:10.1080/00396339708442901

Warren, B. R. (1987). *DOD AND STATE DRAFT REPORTS ON H.R. 2805, CONCERNING THE ESTABLISHMENT OF A COMMISSION TO FOSTER MORE COOPERATIVE PLANNING AND RESPONSE BY OUR NATO AND ASIAN ALLIES TO OUT-OF-AREA THREATS TO WESTERN SECURITY INTERESTS.* (CIA-RDP90M00004R001000080013-5). USA: CIA Retrieved from https://www.cia.gov/library/readingroom/docs/CIA-RDP90M00004R001000080013-5.pdf

Waterman, C. (1985). *US STRATEGIC THINKERS DEBATE PROS AND CONS OF 'PROXY STATES'.* (CIA-RDP90-00965R000807190011-8). Washington D.C.: CIA Retrieved from https://www.cia.gov/library/readingroom/docs/CIA-RDP90-00965R000807190011-8.pdf

Williams, P. (Ed.) (2013). *Security studies : an introduction* (2nd ed.). London: Routledge.

Winrow, G. M. (1993). NATO AND THE OUT-OF-AREA ISSUE: THE POSITIONS OF TURKEY AND ITALY. *Il Politico*, 58(4 (167)), 631-652.

Wörner, M. (1992, March 29). [Opening statement by NATO Secretary General, Manfred Wörner, at the Meeting of Defence Ministers]. Retrieved from https://www.nato.int/cps/su/natohq/official_texts_23995.htm?selectedLocale=en

Wörner, M. (1993a, October 6). ["A New Nato For A New Era": Speech by the Secretary General at the National Press Club Washington, D.C.]. Retrieved from https://www.nato.int/cps/su/natohq/opinions_24171.htm?selectedLocale=en

Wörner, M. (1993b, April 26). [Discours du Secrétaire général de l'OTAN, Manfred Wörner au Forum du Futur]. Retrieved from https://www.nato.int/cps/su/natohq/opinions_24189.htm?selectedLocale=en

Wörner, M. (1993c, November 29). ["Nato and the Weu are Two Viable Building Blocks In Our Broader Effort To Create A New Euro-Atlantic Security Order"]. Retrieved from https://www.nato.int/cps/su/natohq/opinions_24167.htm?selectedLocale=en

Wörner, M. (1993d, October 7). ["NATO: A Changing Alliance for A Changing World" Speech by NATO Secretary General, Mr. Manfred Wörner at the Foreign Policy Association, New York, U.S.A.]. Retrieved from https://www.nato.int/cps/su/natohq/opinions_24170.htm?selectedLocale=en

Wörner, M. (1993e, November 26). [Speech by NATO Secretary General, Manfred Wörner at Inaugural Conference of the Atlantic Council of the United Kingdom]. Retrieved from https://www.nato.int/cps/su/natohq/opinions_24166.htm?selectedLocale=en

Wörner, M. (1993f, May 10). [Speech by NATO Secretary General, Manfred Wörner at the Centro Alti Studi Difesa]. Retrieved from https://www.nato.int/cps/su/natohq/opinions_24186.htm?selectedLocale=en

Wörner, M. (1993g, May 19). [Speech by Secretary General to the International Press Institute]. Retrieved from https://www.nato.int/cps/su/natohq/opinions_24185.htm?selectedLocale=en

Yost, D. S. (1998a). *NATO transformed: the Alliance's new roles in international security*. Washington, D.C.: United States Institute of Peace.

Yost, D. S. (1998b). The new NATO and collective security. *Survival*, 40(2), 135-160. doi:10.1080/00396338.1998.10107846

Yost, D. S. (2010). NATO's evolving purposes and the next Strategic Concept. *International Affairs (Royal Institute of International Affairs 1944-)*, 86(2), 489-522.

www.ingramcontent.com/pod-product-compliance
Lightning Source LLC
Chambersburg PA
CBHW071231240726

48654CB00009B/988